Life: A guide

Andrew Fuller

FINCH PUBLISHING
SYDNEY

For Lucy and Sam

Life: A guide

First published in 2011 in Australia and New Zealand by Finch Publishing Pty Limited, ABN 49 057 285 248, Suite 2207, 4 Daydream Street, Warriewood, NSW, 2102, Australia.

12 11   8 7 6 5 4 3 2

Copyright © 2011 Andrew Fuller

The author asserts his moral rights in this work throughout the world without waiver. All rights reserved. No part of this publication may be reproduced, stored in a retrieval system or transmitted in any form or by any means (electronic or mechanical, through reprography, digital transmission, recording or otherwise) without the prior written permission of the publisher.

National Library of Australia Cataloguing-in-Publication entry:

Fuller, Andrew.
Life: a guide / Andrew Fuller.
9781921462184 (pbk.)
Includes bibliographical references.
Life. Self-actualization (Psychology).
158.1

Edited by Abigail Nathan
Editorial assistance by Tricia Cortez
Text designed and typeset in Stone Serif ITC by Meg Dunworth
Cover design by Ron Monnier
Internal illustrations by Chris Morgan
Printed by BPA Print Group

Notes   The 'Notes' section at the back of this book contains useful additional information and references to quoted material in the text. Each reference is linked to the text by its relevant page number and an identifying line entry.

Disclaimer
While every care has been taken in researching and compiling the information in this book, it is in no way intended to replace professional legal advice and counselling. Readers are encouraged to seek such help as they deem necessary. The authors and publisher specifically disclaim any liability arising from the application of information in this book.

Reproduction and Communication for educational purposes
The Australian Copyright Act 1968 (the Act) allows a maximum of one chapter or 10% of the pages of this work, whichever is the greater, to be reproduced and/or communicated by any educational institution for its educational purposes provided that the educational institution (or the body that administers it) has given a remuneration notice to Copyright Agency Limited (CAL) under the Act. For details of the CAL licence for educational institutions contact: info@copyright.com.au

Finch titles can be viewed and purchased at **www.finch.com.au**

Contents

Navigating your way through life	v
A quick swoop through the stages of life	1
Early years (Ages 0-7)	23
Childhood (Ages 8-14)	35
Adolescence (Ages 15-21)	43
Aspiring adulthood (Ages 22-28)	55
The Napoleon years (Ages 29-35)	77
Clinging to the wreckage (Ages 36-42)	89
Holding the tiger by the tail (Ages 43-49)	105
The agony and the ecstasy (Ages 50-56)	123
Regeneration or degeneration? (Ages 57-63)	135
Intimacy or invisibility? (Ages 64-70)	149
Dignity (Ages 71-77)	159
Contentment and bitterness (Ages 78 and beyond)	169
If I had my life to live over	181
Appendix	199
References	205
Author notes	211
Permissions	222
Acknowledgements	224

Life is a banquet:
but most poor bastards
out there are starving
to death

— Mame.

Navigating your way through life

Once during a ferocious storm at sea, a sailor was tied to a mast. The wild sea tore at the sails and many times the sailor thought all hope was gone and the ship would be lost.

Semi-conscious and battered, the sailor was thrown in all directions by the sea but knew the only hope of survival was to keep clinging to the mast.

Eventually the storm passed and the sea quietened and the sailor's ship was becalmed. Through salt-encrusted eyes the sailor could see the ship was travelling in a gentle circle, driven by the currents.

Looking back over the ocean there was no sign of the way the ship had come to arrive at its current location. Looking towards the open sea stretching to the horizon there was no sign or signal of which was the best way to go forward. Yet for survival it would be necessary to journey onwards. There was not enough water or food on the ship to sustain life.

We are all like the sailor. If we consider our current position in life and look backwards we may well feel entitled to scratch our heads and think, 'How did I get here?' If we look forward to the future there can be an absence of signs or signals about what is the best path to take.

Navigating our way through human life can seem a haphazard and perilous journey. Some days we sail through with a fine breeze. Sometimes we are becalmed and have to reset our course. At other times we scrape on the shoals and reefs that support our existence and we come perilously close to being shipwrecked.

For the most part we assume that we steer the course of our lives. Just as a calm sea may conceal the strong currents beneath, our own willpower and ego can blind us to some of the patterns that drive us and dictate our lives. In order to be happy we should focus more on the trim of our sails than on the winds that blow us about.

This book is about using the wisdom of our ancestors and the rhythm of human development to make your journey though life easier. It's about how to live a good life and understanding what creates resilience at various stages of life.

The seven-year cycle

When I was a boy there was a theory that every seven years, every cell in your body replaced itself. Every seven years you got to be an entirely different person. As a child I found this to be an enchanting idea. Imagine: every seven years getting to be an entirely new person. I excitedly waited for my seventh birthday. I remember waking up early and feeling my skin, which was tingling. I was alive and ready for action.

Now, sadly, the theory about cells replacing themselves completely every seven years didn't turn out to be biologically true. Nevertheless, psychologically and mythologically I think there is a great truth in this theory.

Throughout history people have spoken about seven-year cycles in human life. Michael Apted's *Seven-Up* series of films and the Jesuit adage, 'give me a boy till the age of seven and I will give you the man', are just two examples.

In many cultures the number seven is considered to have special significance. Seven is the number that symbolises the relationship between humanity and the divine. There are seven days in the week, seven colours in a rainbow, seven musical notes, seven orifices in the human body, seven wonders of the world. There are seven theological virtues and, of course, seven deadly sins. In the Christian faith the world was created in seven days. The historical and spiritual allusions to the number seven are numerous (see Appendix on page 199 for a list).

Researching human life, I have worked with thousands of people in workshops, therapy sessions and conferences, and it does seem that many get an opportunity to reflect, re-prioritise and redirect themselves about every seven years.

Many people, every seven years or so, reach a terminus point where they are able to re-orientate their lives. Every seven years there is an opportunity to shift gears and change the way you live your life. It's almost as if we re-invent who we are every seven years.

Shakespeare also referred to the concept of seven when he wrote in *As You Like It* that 'all the world's a stage' and each person plays many parts throughout their lifetime:

> *All the world's a stage,*
> *And all the men and women merely players;*
> *They have their exits and their entrances;*
> *And one man in his time plays many parts,*
> *His acts being seven ages. At first the infant,*
> *Mewling and puking in the nurse's arms;*
> *Then the whining school-boy, with his satchel*
> *And shining morning face, creeping like snail*
> *Unwillingly to school. And then the lover,*
> *Sighing like furnace, with a woeful ballad*
> *Made to his mistress' eyebrow. Then a soldier,*
> *Full of strange oaths, sudden and quick in quarrel,*
> *Seeking the bubble reputation*
> *Even in the cannon's mouth.*
>
> *And then the justice,*
> *In fair round belly with good capon lin'd,*
> *With eyes severe and beard of formal cut,*
> *Full of wise saws and modern instances;*
> *And so he plays his part. The sixth age shifts*
> *Into the lean and slipper'd pantaloon,*

With spectacles on nose and pouch on side,
His youthful hose, well sav'd a world too wide
For his shrunk shank; and his big manly voice,
Turning again toward childish treble, pipes
And whistles in his sound. Last scene of all,
That ends this strange eventful history,
Is second childishness and mere oblivion;
Sans teeth, sans eyes, sans taste, sans every thing.

Of course, not every life neatly fits into this pattern. Random events happen to us all. Life throws up its fair share of unexpected challenges as well as opportunities.

Resilience and life

Resilience is the happy knack of being able to bungy jump through the pitfalls of life. The ability to respond flexibly to whatever life throws at you relies on having the full range of your characteristics at your disposal. This in turn allows you to call upon a range of inner resources to deal with matters at hand.

One of the predictors of a resilient life is our ability to bring different perspectives to a problem. The more points of view we can bring to a situation, the more flexibly we are able to respond to it and the less likely we are to view the problem as insurmountable.

Flexibility is enhanced when you are aware of the inner masculine and feminine aspects of yourself. This is what Carl Jung called the 'anima' (inner feminine) and 'animus' (inner masculine). It is known in Chinese philosophy as the yang and the yin.

Growing up as we do in the presence of men and women, we absorb the ways of handling situations from the opposite sex as well as from our own sex.

Androgyny is the ability to call upon the inner masculine and feminine aspects of yourself to relate flexibly to the world. Being able to deploy those characteristics that are known as masculine such as drive, determination, energy (Yang/ animus) and those that are more usually identified with the feminine (Yin/ anima) gentleness, caring, community allows us great flexibility in responding to the world.

Life patterns

All of the major researchers into human life development have concluded that human life does appear to follow patterns. While there are varying opinions about the names and timings of the phases, there is considerable agreement that human life progresses in set sequences and that these are similar for men and women.

> 'If life is a play it has been badly cast.'
> – Oscar Wilde

Whether your life neatly fits the seven-year pattern or not, it can be a valuable way to look at life. It is still useful to think of life in seven-year chunks. By slicing the human experience into seven-year chunks we can consider what each stage of life requires of us and how to complete it well.

Life is an innovative art and to innovate we need to undergo a process of reinvention of who we are. This flexible way of approaching our lives requires awareness of ourselves and about the patterns of human life. Life has developmental stages. These cannot be accelerated and they are ignored at our peril.

In traditional Indian culture, for example, the phases of life have been described as: self-study till twenty; serving others till forty; teaching till sixty; and travel till eighty.

Confucius summarised his life in the following manner:

> *By thirty I was established, by forty I was without doubt, by fifty I knew my mission in life, by sixty I was undisturbed by anything I heard and by seventy I could follow my wishes without transgressing the way.*

In the wild hurly-burly of life, and in a world that suffers from attention deficit disorder, we place ourselves at risk by ignoring the different stages of life and what might be required to live life to the full.

The art of living life well

The art of living life well is the most distinguished of all the arts. This book is about living well and having a great life. Not what it takes to become rich in a monetary sense but what is takes to be wealthy from the most vital treasure you have: your life.

There are many theories about life. One of my favourites comes from a group of students who were sitting around thinking about life. Together they came up with a fantastic idea which became known as the backwards theory of life.

> *You start out dead and you get that out of the way.*
> *Then you wake up in an old age home feeling better every day.*
> *You get kicked out for being too healthy.*
> *So you go on the pension and when you finally start work they give you a gold watch on your first day.*
> *You work for forty years until you are young enough to enjoy your retirement.*
> *Then you party and have a wild time, get to have lots*

of sex when you really, really want it, until you are ready to start high school.
You play, have no responsibilities, you become a kid, you go to primary school.
Then you become a baby.
You spend your last nine months floating in a spa with central heating and room service on tap and a small doof machine in the background.
And then ... (this is the best bit!)
You finish off as an orgasm!

As a theory of life I think it has a lot going for it.

Woody Allen once said, 'I don't want to achieve immortality through my work. I want to achieve it through not dying.' While we also might secretly wish this, being aware that life is a limited resource and that death awaits all of us can bring vibrancy to our lives.

There is a surprising lack of guidelines about how to live life well as an adult. The holy scriptures provide guidance to the devout but in the non-secular world things are a bit sketchy. Developmental theorists have described the stages of childhood well. Some have outlined the teenage years. However, when we get to the bulk of human life things get blurry. These years are often dismissed as 'adulthood, old age and death'. Even the famous developmental psychologist Erik Erikson described the whole of adulthood as a thirty-year-long developmental stage and asserted that it was about generativity versus stagnation. This is not especially helpful for someone trying to navigate their way through these years.

When an acorn falls to the ground it has all the information it needs to become an oak tree. Unlike the oak, humans have the code to develop physically but need additional information to develop psychologically into a full adult. This information is contained in our culture and family histories. It is also retained in our unconscious minds as archetypes and memes, which are ideas and concepts that have evolved over human history. Regardless of our own individual perspectives, there are characteristic ways in which humans view the world.

The stories that people tell one another reflect the issues they face. The stories that have been told about human lives are remarkably similar across cultures and across the centuries. Theorist Carl Jung argued that people are constructed psychologically in essentially the same way so that the same types of thoughts, experiences and perceptions reoccur in many lives. One example of a recurring theme is that over 1000 variations of the Cinderella story have been collected. Author Christopher Booker argues that there are only seven basic plots for all the stories ever told: tragedy, comedy, rags to riches, overcoming the monster, the quest, rebirth and voyage and return.

The direct relevance of these stories and patterns is not always in our awareness and is not even obvious, which is not particularly useful for someone trying to use them to create a great life. Which is why in the waiting room of my clinical practice there is a sign that reads:

> **This is not your real life.**
>
> **This is a test.**
>
> **If it was your real life, you would've received better instructions.**

The rituals, rites and customs that are used to signify major changes in life in tribal societies have been discarded. In the Western world they have been replaced by servitude to the clock and an anxious anticipation of what is about to happen next.

Many people are too busy to clearly plan their future, too time poor to reflect on their past and ancestry, and too distracted to enjoy the experience of the moment. This book tries to help find yardsticks and markers for navigating the journey that is human life and some suggestions for getting the best out of it. While it is worth being clear about the destination, it is the journey, and what you do with it, which makes it worthwhile.

> 'What a caterpillar calls the end, the rest of the world calls a butterfly.'
> – Lao Tsu

A quick swoop through the stages of life

Above a square in Ravella in the year 1308, where the coos of pigeons and the snorting and snuffling of passing horses was almost deafening, Durante degli Alighieri inked his quill. Musing on the forty-three eventful years of his life and his circumstances as an exile, Dante began the first line of his epic poem, 'The Divine Comedy', with a dilemma that had plagued many before him and would continue to perplex many who came after:

> *Midway upon the journey of our life*
> *I found myself within a forest dark,*
> *For the straightforward pathway had been lost.*

Across history we find many examples of times in human lives when the road ahead became obscured and the purpose of the journey was uncertain. These times can be fraught with confusion. Just as there are times of confusion and disarray in life, there are times of opportunity and power.

There are times in our lives when being purposeful and goal-directed serves us well. But there are also times when we should pause with eager attention, rather like a hunting dog with a paw raised, waiting for the next sign. There are moments in our lives when the best thing we can do is to sit quietly and wait to see who or what shows up.

There is much we can learn from history's main players that can inform us about how to discover our own paths and live our lives. One hundred years before Dante, Giovanni Francesco Bernardone heard a sermon that would change his life. The age of twenty-eight was for Giovanni, as it has been for so many others, a time of clarity about his purpose and mission in life. On 24 February 1209 Giovanni changed his name to Francis of Assisi, and decided, no doubt to his father's chagrin, to devote his life to living in poverty and undertaking good works.

At about the same time as Dante was composing 'The Divine Comedy', a twelve-year-old girl living in the small village of Domremy, France, began to hear voices. These voices instructed her to support the French king against the English in the Hundred Years War. A few years later, at the age of sixteen, she offered her services to the French king and Joan of Arc turned the tide of history.

Nearly 300 years after Dante, William Shakespeare sat down to contemplate not only his own life at age thirty-seven, but also the fate of an ailing Queen Elizabeth I, who had no clear heirs or successors. The slime, stink and salt of the tidal river near Southwark in London must have entered his nostrils as he pondered both their fates. The continuity of leadership and the succession of power were uncertain for the monarchy of England. Shakespeare saw a parallel in the turbulent times of Julius Caesar and penned the lines:

*There is a tide in the affairs of men
Which, taken at the flood, leads on to fortune;
Omitted, all the voyage of their life
Is bound in shallows and miseries
On such a full sea are we now afloat
And we must take the current when it serves,
Or lose our ventures.*

Shakespeare's writing mirrors the dilemma of many people in their late thirties: how to capitalise on opportunities and the tides of fortune. The images of pathways and tidal rivers well suit the human experience of life. Twisting and turning and rising and ebbing; our lives bob along seemingly wayward, uncontrollable and erratic.

But is it as uncertain and as shiftable as it seems? Can we make any sense at all of the tumble of moments and experiences that we call life, or is it simply a random collage of unpredictable twists and turns? Are there patterns that determine the stages of our lives?

The idea of a self-determined life, so popular in modern self-help texts, is a relatively new one. Popular and best-selling titles such as *Feel the Fear and Do It Anyway*, and *You Can Achieve Anything You Want*, applaud rugged individualism and persistence, some might even say pig-headed self-centredness. Even the great playwright, Anton Chekov subscribed to this view. 'Tell me what you want and I will tell you what you are,' he reportedly said.

For most of history, our ancestors did not view life as controlled by choice. The ancient Greeks and Romans explained their circumstances as whims of the Gods, Muses, fates or destiny. Much of the Asian- and Spanish-speaking world still agrees with them.

Our current perspective is that people can actively choose their life circumstances. That life is something which is completely shaped by our decisions may seem empowering but it can also be a source of blame. If we have financial problems, we may be told that we are yet to find the key to success. If we have difficulties in love, we are told to 'play the game' or follow a set of prescribed rules or strategies that seem to take us away from intimacy rather than towards it.

Despite the current view that our situations are largely controlled by individual choice, the most fundamental aspects of our lives are not within our power to choose. We don't choose our parents, our bodies, our temperament or our talents. What we do choose, especially as we mature, is the way we approach the circumstances in our lives. In order to understand the best approach, it is important to have an awareness of the different stages and patterns of life, especially if we want to capitalise on the highs and successfully navigate the lows.

A master class from some of history's giants

When we learn about the stages of human life and what each requires of us we are in a much more powerful position to catch those tides of opportunity. To do this, let's take a quick ramble through history to see if those who have trodden the path before us can help to light the way. Let's see if the eventful lives of some of history's key players tell us anything about the overall patterns of human life.

While the situations faced by many of history's main figures differ, the challenges they met at various ages bear similarities. Of course the people who, historically, we know most about are exceptional people, but even so, there may be lessons for all of us in how they managed the changes in their lives.

Teenagers

Across history, tentatively or boldly, teenagers leap into life. If you happened to be around the art studio of Andrea del Verrocchio in Florence in the year 1466, you might have been able to catch a glimpse of a young fourteen-year-old nervously beginning the first day of his apprenticeship. It was the beginning of a wonderful career. The apprentice's designs and artworks became known across the world and are priceless today. The career of Leonardo da Vinci had begun.

Of course history is littered with accounts of youthful hi-jinks and adventures. If the high seas, salt and seagulls make your heart soar, you could have loped down to the docks and gone off to sea with the seventeen-year-old authors-to-be Joseph Conrad or Jack London. On the streets of Paris, the cadent tones of seventeen-year-old Edith Piaf beginning her singing career could be heard. If you slipped quietly into a Harlem nightclub you could have caught the mellow sounds of the blues as Billie Holiday, also seventeen, began to weave her magic.

The lure of foreign adventure appeals to many. Rudyard Kipling set out to work as a journalist and, some say, spy in India. If the dusty by-ways of the subcontinent don't appeal, perhaps you might have dropped in on the nineteen-year-old Ernest Hemingway as he sped around as an ambulance driver in World War 1.

If it's feistiness and the determination of youth you are looking for it is hard to go past Eleanor of Aquitaine who, at the age of nineteen, defied her husband King Louis VII of France and the Pope and went on the crusades. She divorced at age thirty and married the future King Henry II of England, who eventually imprisoned her. Living to a ripe old age she reflected:

> *The many bends along the highroad of my life conceal the vistas between this fleeting moment of pure being and ancient recollections coursing like deerhounds through my head. In a life of four score years and more, who can look so far back? The very richness of experience crowds and clouds the brains.*

For others the mantle of responsibility and obligation falls on their shoulders early. In their late teens or very early twenties Catherine the Great, Lorenzo de Medici, Mary Queen of Scots and Alexander the Great all became rulers.

Power and responsibility can be heavy burdens if you are too young. Not all were able to hold onto their power. In 1492 you could have ridden at breakneck speed up the hills to the south of Granada to a place known as 'the pass of the Moor's sigh' or Puerto del Suspiro del Moro with Boabdil, King of Granada. Looking over the magnificence of the Alhambra that he was surrendering to the Christians, he wept. His mother reproached him. 'Don't weep like a woman for what you could not defend as a man.' Tough words for a young man of twenty-two to hear.

The twenties

The twenties are often a time of working out whether to follow traditions or to forge your own path. The decision to follow the conventional routes or to strike out on his own must have weighed upon Bill Gates' mind as he dropped out of Harvard and co-founded a risky new company called Microsoft. By thirty he was the world's youngest billionaire and later became one of the great benefactors in history.

While following conventions in your twenties can appear less courageous, forging your own path can easily get you labelled as a troublemaker or a maverick. If you had been around in 1964 you might have met an eloquent young man creating his own destiny. Born with a slave-name, Cassius Clay Junior was to join the Nation of Islam and change his name to Muhammad Ali at twenty-two years of age. He became the first man to win the world heavyweight championship three times. In 1967 Ali refused to enter the draft for the war in Vietnam due to his religious beliefs. He was stripped of his championship title and his boxing licence was suspended. Ali did not fight again for nearly four years.

The early twenties are a time of identity formation for many and, for those who gain a sense of who they are early on, the creativity and vitality of this age has been used to great effect. Both Mary Shelley, author of *Frankenstein*, and Jane Austen, author of *Pride and Prejudice*, created their most significant works in this time. It was during their twenties that Charles Lindbergh, pioneer aviator, learned to fly, Plato became a disciple of Socrates and Ivan the Great became Grand Prince of Moscow.

Travel seduces the adventurous during the twenties, often with tremendous outcomes. At this stage of life, Charles Darwin began his voyages of the *Beagle*, Virginia Woolf moved to Bloomsbury, Ernest Hemingway moved to Paris and Harry Houdini tried out travel of a different kind by escaping from a hospital straitjacket. In 1951 at the age of twenty-three young medical student, Che Guevara, from the University of Buenos Aires, started a motorcycle trip across South America. The poverty he witnessed on the way greatly inspired the future revolutionary.

When your father executes your mother, the family dynamics are not going well. When your half-sister places you in the same prison where your mother was killed, all is not rosy. So it is no surprise that Queen Elizabeth I of England may have looked upon the intentions of others warily. At the age of twenty-five, upon hearing that her half-sister had died and the throne was hers, she reportedly quoted the 118th Psalm from the Bible: 'It is the Lord's doing and it is marvellous in our eyes.' She was to rule with steely determination in a time when many doubted the capacity of women to be effective monarchs.

If you had been looking down the dusty main street of Springfield, Missouri, on 21 July 1865, you would have seen two men focusing intently on each other. Pistols in hands, the men were about to have the first ever showdown. Some say it was over a woman, others say it was a watch and gambling debts that did it. Whatever the cause, Davis Tutt Junior and James Butler Hickock faced off, 75 yards apart. Tutt was the better marksman but his shot missed. Hickok did not falter and he shot Tutt in the side, killing him. Consequently, at the age of twenty-eight, with considerable self-promotion, the legend of Wild Bill Hickock was launched.

Another man with a talent for self-promotion also saw the need for a more inspirational title than François-Marie Arouet. At the age of twenty-four, in 1718, he chose as his nom de plume a name that suggested speed and daring and became the famous commentator, essayist and philosopher Voltaire.

So the twenties are a time in which life is to be grasped. Opportunities are there to be taken, if you are fortunate enough to be bold and are certain of your character.

The thirties

The formation of identity and achievement in the late twenties and early thirties can topple people into directions they least expect. It is almost as if it takes until you are nearly thirty to fully detach from childhood circumstances so you can make your way in the world under your own steam.

For Siddhartha, twenty-nine was the age to leave his royal life and family to take on the lifestyle of a seeker and ascetic. At the age of thirty-five he attained enlightenment and became the Buddha or 'awakened one'. According to many sources, Jesus also began preaching his ministry at age thirty.

At the age of thirty, in 1905, Carl Jung had his first discussion with Sigmund Freud, a conversation lasting thirteen hours, which marked an investigation into how the fragile human conscious life is determined by mysterious and unconscious forces.

A world away, a former leader of a gang of bandits was undergoing a personal transformation of her own. After surviving an abusive childhood and seeking revenge on authority, Phoolan Devi, perhaps better known as the Bandit Queen of India, created a new career for herself at age thirty-one. After languishing in jail for leading her gang in violent massacres, Phoolan was elected to Parliament.

Inspiration and imagination during the thirties can change the world. At thirty-one, Germaine Greer wrote *The Female Eunuch* and accelerated the women's movement. At the same age, Antoni Gaudi began work designing the Sagrada Familia, the still-to-be completed cathedral in Barcelona.

For those who combine clarity of vision with action, the determination of the early thirties can be remarkable. If you had been in the vicinity of the Doge's Palace in Venice in the swirling fog on Halloween, 1757, you may have caught sight of a figure escaping by gondola. Casanova attributed his success in life to his ability to concentrate on a single goal until it yielded. When pursuing a woman he thought of nothing else. When imprisoned in the Doge's Palace in Venice, a prison from which no-one escaped, he concentrated on the single goal of escape. A change of cells, which meant that months of digging had all been for nothing, did not discourage him; he persisted and eventually escaped. 'I have always believed,' he later wrote in his memoirs, 'that when a man gets it into his head to do something and when he exclusively occupies himself in that design, he must succeed whatever the difficulties.'

The early thirties have been a time of enterprise for many. In 1854 the British press reported the appalling conditions endured by wounded soldiers in the Crimean War. As a result, at the age of thirty-four Florence Nightingale had found her mission. She recruited and equipped a team of nurses and went to Turkey to help the hurt and wounded.

The mid-thirties often sees a power surge in people's lives. Energy is high. Resources are frequently at a peak and new ventures and undertakings are embarked upon. At the age of thirty-six, Maria Montessori opened her first Casa di Bambini, a school for children; Sylvia Pankhurst campaigned for women's suffrage; Georges Bizet composed *Carmen* in 1875; Oscar Wilde performed his first play, *Lady Windermere's Fan*; George Eliot wrote her first novel and John Cleese created *Fawlty Towers*.

The power surge of the thirties can also be accompanied by the seeds of discontent.

If you had visited the low income housing of Chicago in 1927, you might have chanced upon a heartbroken and unemployed architect mourning the death of his daughter. Using alcohol as his prop, Buckminster Fuller was blurrily contemplating suicide. During his dark night of the soul, he resolved instead to live out the rest of his life as an experiment to see what one person could do to help humanity. The architect and inventor of the geodesic dome went on to contribute many influential ideas over his lifespan.

In 1926 one of the most successful detective novelists was involved in a mystery of her own. Her car was found abandoned close to her home in Surrey and her bag of clothes was within. Her disappearance at age thirty-six received widespread media coverage. Two of her fellow authors, Dorothy L. Sayers and Sir Arthur Conan Doyle, were drafted to assist in the search. For eleven days a nationwide search ensued. If you had peered into the dining room at the Swan Hydro Hotel in Yorkshire you might have spotted Agatha Christie who had booked herself into the hotel under the alias of 'Neele' (which by no coincidence was also the surname of her husband's mistress).

If you had been in a tavern in inner London in 1746 you might have met a tall, rambunctious, opinionated, verbose man making wild claims about completing a dictionary of the entire English language within three years. The thirty-five-year-old Samuel Johnson was perhaps a bit too bold in his assertion; it actually took him nine years to complete.

Of course ill health and setbacks can strike any of us at any time. On 4 July 1939, a ceremony was held to honour Lou Gehrig whose record of 2130 games of baseball came to an end with the onset of a crippling disease. His speech at the time illustrates that living well is not just about what life serves up for us but what we make of it:

> *Fans, for the past two weeks you have been reading about a bad break I got. Yet today I consider myself the luckiest man on the face of the earth. I have been in ballparks for*

seventeen years and have never received anything but kindness and encouragement from you fans ...

Sure, I'm lucky. When the New York Giants, a team you would give your right arm to beat, and vice versa, sends you a gift, that's something! When everybody down to the groundskeepers and those boys in white coats remember you with trophies, that's something.

When you have a wonderful mother-in-law who takes sides with you in squabbles against her own daughter, that's something. When you have a father and mother who work all their lives so that you can have an education

When you have a wife who has been a tower of strength and shown more courage than you dreamed existed, that's the finest I know.

So I close in saying that I might have had a tough break – but I have an awful lot to live for.

The age of thirty-six is often a time of great expansion in many people's lives and so it has been for many of history's main players. On 10 September 1946, a nun who worked as a schoolteacher was on a train journey back to Darjeeling when she received a directive from God that she was to have the courage to work with the poorest of the poor. For Mother Teresa, 'It was a command I had to obey.'

At the same age, Stanley Kubrick directed his anti-war film *Dr Strangelove*, and Yasser Arafat, Palestinian leader, oversaw a rapid expansion of his guerrilla movement al-Fatah. Louis Armstrong became internationally famous as a jazz musician.

In their later thirties Francis Drake circumnavigated the world and Cole Porter wrote 'Let's Do It', later voted the most popular song of the 20th century. There is a surge of creative undertakings in this phase of life. At around this age Charles Dickens wrote *David Copperfield*, Dian Fossey became the first primatologist to be accepted by mountain gorillas, Robert Fulton developed the steamboat, physicist Georg

Simon Ohm discovered Ohm's Law and Neil Armstrong became the first person to walk on the moon. Roz Savage rowed solo across the Atlantic Ocean. This adventure was inspired by a writing exercise in which she wrote two versions of her obituary: one in which she had lived a conventional life, and another in which she had lived the life she wanted to have.

For some the energy and vitality of purpose that accompanies the early thirties often wanes in the late thirties. It can be a time of clinging to the wreckage. At the age of thirty-eight Jean Paul Satre wrote, 'Man is a useless passion,' and 'Everything that exists is born for no reason, carries on living through weakness and dies by accident.'

The forties

The forties are often a turbulent time. Life is busy. Demands are many. Ambition is strong. You can feel like you are holding a tiger by its tail.

If you had been on a bus in Montgomery, Alabama, in the mid-1950s, where you sat would have depended on the colour of your skin. Blacks at the back, whites up front. That was the rule. At least it was until 1 December 1955, when Rosa Parks, aged forty-two, refused to obey bus driver James Blake's order that she give up her seat to make room for a white passenger. Parks's act of defiance became an important symbol of the modern Civil Rights Movement.

If you had wandered around Boston in the early 1920s you may have met a man of Lebanese heritage who at the age of forty published a book that was picked up by counter-culturalists forty years later. Khalil Gibran's *The Prophet* has remained in print ever since.

At the age forty-two Fillippo Brunelleschi had a problem. No-one since antiquity had built a dome as large as the one he had proposed for the Florence Cathedral. The great dome of the Pantheon in Rome was an example but the formula for the concrete mix had long since been forgotten. There was nothing for it – the dome would have to be built out of bricks. He'd won the competition to construct the dome using an incomplete model helped out by Donatello. Winning the competition had been a near thing. Completing the dome was even more of a trial.

Ingeniously he came up with an octagonal design of the double-walled dome, resting on a drum and not on the roof itself. Brunelleschi had to invent special hoisting machines to complete the dome. Work started on the dome in 1420 and was completed in 1436.

Napoleon Bonaparte did not have the best of times during his forties. After a career of brilliant military victories achieved through strategy, concealment of troop deployments and focusing his attacks on the enemy's weakened fronts, it is fair to say that Napoleon bit off more than he could chew. The invasion of Russia resulted in only 10 per cent of his troops surviving and returning to France. The rest perished at the hands of the Russian army, starved, or froze to death in the freezing conditions. His loss at the Battle of Waterloo only three years later was devastating and resulted in his exile to St Helena, 2000 kilometres from any land mass.

If you had been a sailor in the seas off Spain in 1805, you would have received the dour message that 'England expects every man to do his duty', and you may well have prepared for the worst. The English fleet faced the might of thirty-three of France's and Spain's largest warships. Admiral Horatio Nelson, using the cunning of all of his forty-seven years, set his fleet to the side of the enemy's ships with the intention of breaking through their lines and separating their fleet. Unconventional as it was, the strategy worked and the Battle of Trafalgar was won. While Nelson was able to minimise casualties on his side, his own was not among the lives he saved.

In late 1916, Grigori Yefimovich Rasputin sat down to write a letter in which he not only accurately predicted his own death at age forty-seven but also the entire Romanov family within two years. This was no idle prediction from a man who had already survived an attempted poisoning, suffocation, four bullet wounds and a beating before a drowning finally finished him off.

The late forties and early fifties is a time of crisis or reinvention in many people's lives.

It was at the age of forty-nine in 335 BC that Aristotle returned to Athens and established his own school known as the Lyceum. In the following years he contributed to so many areas of life that he has been thought of as the last person to know everything there was to be known in his lifetime.

At the same age of forty-nine, Eleanor Roosevelt had a problem. She experienced as many do, the agony and the ecstasy of this time of life. Her paraplegic husband had won the US Presidency and her marriage was imperilled by dalliances on both sides. She had the choice of becoming an ornamental First Lady and feeling useless or defying the customs of the time and pursuing a busy schedule of speaking engagements. She chose the latter and played a powerful role in race relations and women's rights.

If you had been with Leo Tolstoy as he completed *Anna Karenina* you may have felt concerned. Despite having created one of the great works of literature, Tolstoy, horrified by the meaninglessness of existence, experienced bouts of depression and considered suicide. He finally embraced the idea of living life according to his conscience, including the renunciation of all forms of violence, the lessening of material possessions, the simple faith of the peasants and universal love.

The fifties

The early fifties are a time during which people can place themselves in peril. In the Jazz Age of 1927, the most notorious dancer of her age flung a flowing scarf around her neck and stepped into the passenger seat of a sports car. As the car sped along the roads of Nice, the scarf became entangled in the open-spoked wheels of the car and wrenched Isadora Duncan, aged fifty, to her death. Gertrude Stein upon hearing of the freakish death commented dryly, 'Affectations can be dangerous.'

Isadora joined a fine company of rabble-rousers, including Errol Flynn, Dee Dee Ramone, Michael Jackson and Antoine Lavoisier, who discovered too late that fifty can be a very dangerous age to be.

The resolution of the crisis that often accompanies the late forties and early fifties often brings forth new directions and possibilities. For Abraham Lincoln it involved overcoming a life of setbacks and disappointments that included failures in business, a nervous breakdown at twenty-five and so many defeats at the polls that many would have been tempted to whisper in his ear, 'Abe, face it you're not going to win, give up and go easy on yourself.' If anyone did advise him to give up he clearly didn't accept it. At the age of fifty-one he was elected as the President of the United States of America.

For many the late fifties and sixties bring seniority and clarity of ideals. For many it is a time of conviction.

At the age of fifty, you were now old enough to be the head of the curia (200 BC), the original assembly and forerunner of the Senate in early Roman times.

If you had been in the Karntnerortheater in Vienna in 1824 you might have found yourself nudging a famous composer in the ribs and yelling into his ear, 'Hey, stop conducting, Ludwig, the audience are applauding.' Ludwig van Beethoven completed his *Ninth Symphony* despite being so deaf that, at the end of its first performance at age fifty-three, he could not hear when the audience was applauding.

If you had been in the Tower of London in 1535, and be thankful you were not, you may have tried to convince a man of fifty-seven years that his cause was a foolish one. Cajoling him into signing an oath that recognised King Henry the Eighth as the Supreme Head of the Church of England you may have suggested, 'Surely, as a former Chancellor of England you of all people know the law can be shifted. Look at how swiftly and sneakily Cromwell swept away the freedom of the Church, a law that had stood since the Magna Carta.' All of your arguments would have failed to convince the resolute Sir Thomas More who was later executed in the Tower.

At the age of fifty-seven, another man of conviction also had to face the inevitable. If you had been standing beside Mangus on 3 September 1886 you would have seen a man trying to do the best by his people. After a year of seeking freedom in the lands they originally called their own, Mangus, also known as Geronimo, leader of the Chiricahua Apaches, was forced to concede to the white man.

If you had been in Berlin on 9 November 1989 you would have viewed something almost unimaginable in the previous decade. Through the bravery and courage of Soviet leader Mikhail Gorbachev, age fifty-eight, the fall of the Berlin Wall and the re-unification of Germany was achieved.

There is often a new surge of life force throughout the late fifties. At fifty-six, Mao Zedong founded the Peoples' Republic of China, JS Bach fathered the last of his twenty children and Handel wrote *The Messiah*. Bernini started constructing the piazza and colonnade at the front of St Peters in Rome at the age of fifty-seven. English novelist and journalist Daniel Defoe wrote his first and most famous novel, *The Life and Adventures of Robinson Crusoe*, at fifty-nine.

The sixties

The twists and turns of life can be poignant in the mid-sixties. If you had been on the riverbank opposite one of India's most important buildings in 1658 you would have felt the sorrow. As if losing his beloved wife in childbirth wasn't enough, Shah Jahan (literally King of the World) had the double misfortune of being imprisoned by his son. He was to spend the rest of his life in captivity across from the monument he had constructed in his wife's memory, the Taj Mahal.

Mahatma Gandhi started on his salt marches at the age of sixty in 1930, commencing a long journey towards independence for India from British rule.

In 1984, aged sixty-six years, one of the most successful politicians of her age made a decision that would cost her her life. Indira Gandhi ordered her army to fire upon the holiest shrine in the Sikh world, the Golden Temple at Amritsar. Gandhi was concerned that Sikh separatists were stockpiling weapons there. Four months later Indira was shot and killed by her Sikh bodyguards.

For some, the mid-sixties bring the poignancy of loss and invisibility, for others it is a time of intimacy, even if it is mainly with one's own memories. In 1792 Giacomo Casanova finished the first draft of his memoirs of a life well lived. Exiled in Bohemia, the Venetian reflected on sixty-seven full years of life that included stints as a healer, pimp, gourmand, flirt, violinist, clergyman, spy, con man, lawyer, playwright, mathematician, military officer and even a failed attempt to turn the Marquess d'Urfe from a woman into a young man. Reflecting on his life as perhaps history's most notorious lover, Casanova noted that he was writing about his life to laugh at himself and he was succeeding.

The seventies

The dignity, conviction and fearless determination of the latter years is well exemplified by the seventy-one-year-old Golda Meir, Prime Minister of Israel. She led the country though the Yom Kippur War in 1973, which was over occupied lands taken by Israel in 1967. The re-taking of these lands by Egypt and Syria was to shape Middle Eastern politics for decades to come.

In 399 BC, around the age of seventy, Socrates was accused of offending public morality. Despite being able to easily negotiate his way out of the charge, Socrates declared his own contentment with his conduct and the sentence. Echoing thoughts similar to the Buddha's, Socrates is reported to have commented that, 'To want nothing is divine, to want as little as possible is the nearest approach to the divine life'. Socrates was sentenced to death by drinking hemlock and was killed as much by his own convictions as anything else.

The senior years of life can bring great contentment and joy. Leo Tolstoy celebrated his seventieth birthday by riding twenty miles and making love to his wife, having overcome his earlier depression.

The years from forty-five to seventy-two are an enormous slice of life. If you were pacing it away in a prison you may well become bitter. However, following his release from prison on 11 February 1990, Nelson Mandela supported reconciliation and negotiation, and helped lead the transition towards multi-racial democracy in South Africa and became President. Mandela was awarded the Nobel Peace Prize in 1993.

On his seventieth birthday Mark Twain made a speech. Here is an extract:

> *The seventieth birthday! It is the time of life when you arrive at a new and awful dignity; when you may throw aside the decent reserves which have oppressed you for a generation and stand unafraid and unabashed upon your seven-terraced summit and look down and teach – unrebuked. You can tell the world how you got there ...*
>
> *'I have achieved my seventy years in the usual way: by sticking strictly to a scheme of life which would kill anybody else. It sounds like an exaggeration, but that is really the common rule for attaining to old age. ...*
>
> *I have been persistently strict in sticking to the things which didn't agree with me until one or the other of us got the best of it ...*
>
> *... We can't reach old age by another man's road. My habits protect my life, but they would assassinate you ...*

The creativity of the advanced years should never be underestimated. These are the years like childhood, when people have time to spare and energy to burn. If our minds are active and broadened and we seek to involve ourselves in love and life, the vitality and inspiration stay with us.

The eighties
The renowned writer and thinker Johann Wolfgang von Goethe finished writing *Faust* at eighty-two. At age ninety, Marc Chagall became the first living artist to be exhibited at the Louvre museum. Pablo Picasso was still producing drawings and engravings and the chemist Paul Walden was still giving chemistry lectures well into his nineties.

The patterns of life

So what can we conclude from this kaleidoscope of history? For many of us life has a pattern. It is a pattern that begins in the wonder of childhood, stretches awkwardly in adolescence, surges forth with great energy and busy endeavour in early adulthood, before grinding towards a yearning for greater meaning in mid life. If attained, this meaning leads us towards creativity, compassion and eventually to a deep connection with the world.

Life is a work in progress. It is the most essential of the improvisational arts. Life is rich and indeed it is short. As Crowfoot (1821–1890), the Blackfoot Native American, observed, 'What is life? It is the flash of a firefly in the night. It is the breath of a buffalo in the wintertime. It is the little shadow which runs across the grass and loses itself in the sunset.'

Human life has seasons and cycles. These cycles reverberate across history and have resonated for generations. Most of us have the illusion that life is totally within our control. All we need to do is to get smarter, richer, thinner or become more beautiful and the prize of happiness and contentment ever after will be ours. Despite this, most people are, most of the time, flying by the seat of their pants. If we look at life at all, it is a sidelong glance and we look away quickly and fearfully from the prospect of death. This denial does not serve us well.

Knowing the likely cycles of life is like reading a map. It can let us know the signposts, the probable pitfalls, the terrain we need to cover, as well as moments when we should stop, pause and take in the beauty of the view.

From the moment of birth, death is inevitable and from the moment of death, life is also inevitable. This is the dance of existence. In the Hindu tradition this is encapsulated in the Hindu god Shiva, who is simultaneously creator and destroyer. No loss without gain and no gain without loss. This is beautifully conveyed in two lines from the poet Dylan Thomas, 'I felt the pulse of summer in the ice,' and, 'The tree is felled in the acorn.'

Humans are no exception to the rhythms of existence but they think they are. Ignoring these patterns condemns people, as author F. Scott Fitzgerald put it, to 'beat on, boats against the current, being borne back ceaselessly into the past.'

One of the key aspects of living life well is to be able to anticipate what will be needed to thrive in the next phase of your life. Being able to plan for and create solutions for your future means that you benefit from being aware of the patterns and demands of the phases of life. By studying how other people have lived their lives, we gain the advantage of being able to look a little further down the road. As Isaac Newton would have had it, we will be able to see further by standing on the shoulders of giants.

Early years (Ages 0-7)

There is said to be a secret behind every baby's first cry. According to legend, before birth the baby is told that there is one thing they must learn this time around. However, the moment the baby is born, they forget what it is. The baby cries, 'Alas, I have forgotten.'

The way we are loved in our early years shapes us as individually and uniquely as our fingerprints. It forms the basis of the way we react to life and the way we consider death. It determines our degree of cautiousness or daring. It dictates how we respond to threats and the way that we love. For many people the way we were loved, or not loved enough, early in our lives can lead to problems with attachment and belonging, and can leave us with a sense of abandonment. Unless we take time to recalibrate our early pattern of love and belonging, this sense of abandonment may resonate throughout our lives.

Repeating negative patterns

Many people's sense of abandonment shows up most vividly at times of ritual and family gathering. In the Western world these times traditionally include birthdays, Easter, Thanksgiving and Christmas. You may recognise a sense of abandonment in the relative for whom the gift is never big enough, the turkey not cooked in quite the right way or who becomes upset when the greeting is insufficiently cheery. And, because they are unaware of what they are doing, they repeat the same dreaded pattern, year after mind-blistering year.

It is often easier to see the flaws of others than the imperfections in ourselves but we all share the wound of being let down in one way or another throughout our early years. No matter how loving our parents were, no parent can instantly be there for every nappy change, burp, gurgle or peek-a-boo game. So we all get a bit let down as infants. This disappointment causes a division of the self into two parts:

> 'If you want your children to be brilliant read them fairy stories. If you want them to be even more brilliant read them more fairy stories.' – Albert Einstein

- Your true self; and
- Your critical self.

Your true self is the part of you that just does life – it doesn't want to comment on it, evaluate or reflect upon it; it just wants to get on with living life.

Your critical self is the part of you that wants to run a commentary about how well (or not) you are doing whatever you are doing. Your critical self has an opinion about everything! Your critical self chatters away, making never-ending comments on how well you are doing. It niggles, corrects and cajoles you; and it gets in the way of your performance. Your critical self raises your anxiety levels.

If your critical self gets out of control you risk suffering from perfectionism and/or paralysis through not daring to risk trying out new ventures. One of the ways to alleviate people from the tyranny of the critical self is to focus on the experience of completing activities, rather than focusing on the result. This is also known as mindfulness.

The ways we express the insecurities developed by experiences in our early years determine the way we deal with threats and times of trouble. Many people repeat the same patterns over and over again, especially in their relationships. Unless we step back and recalibrate our early sense of belonging we will repeat the same behaviour over and over with different people and feel perplexed and helpless in the face of the relentless repetition of life. We sentence ourselves to living a life that continuously revolves around the dose of love and attachment we received early on.

The source of all power

There are many places of power in the world – the Pentagon, the Vatican, Downing Street, the Kremlin – but the most powerful of all is the family home. The family is the most powerful structure of human belonging in the world. It is the place where gifts are received – gifts that take a lifetime to unwrap. It is sadly also the place where wounds can be inflicted that take a lifetime to heal.

As young children we all had some hard lessons to learn. There is no union without separation. No return without parting. No belonging is permanent. These are essential lessons but it is important not to learn them too soon. Learning these lessons too harshly or too early wounds the baby and leaves the emerging person insecure, anxious and disillusioned.

It is difficult to love yourself if you are not first loved. Our parents give us the language through which we see the world. This is why it is important to protect children as much as possible from the horrors and uncertainties of the world.

Even so, parents do not have to be the perfect providers and nurturers. Humans are a resilient lot and infants have basic survival needs: nutrition, sleep, security, love and play.

Babies are as smart as they can be. They know what they need to know and are very effective and selective about getting the information they need. They are designed to learn about the world through play and especially with the people who love them.

Babies stare intently at complex images (stripes, corners and faces) and neglect expensive toys. The intrigue shown by babies is that of an investigator. They are busy figuring out how the world works. Babies are trying to read minds and intentions.

One of the most important questions in a baby's mind is what causes things to happen. This is very important for a baby's survival because they rely on having other people do things for them. Infancy is a long experiment based on the question, if I do this, what will happen next? If I gurgle or cry

> 'I think the splendor of my childhood was unique because it was absolute poverty but also absolute freedom; out in the open, surrounded by trees, animals, apparitions and people who were indifferent toward me. My existence was not even justified, nobody cared. This gave me an incredible opportunity to escape it all without anyone worrying where I was or when I would return. I used to climb trees, and everything seemed much more beautiful from up there. I could embrace the world in its completeness and feel a harmony that I could not experience down below, with the clamor of my aunts, the cursing of my grandfather, or the cackling of the hens ... Trees have a secret life that is only revealed to those willing to climb them.' – Reinaldo Arenas

out, do I get a different response? Eventually, babies resolve this to their satisfaction by deciding that they cause everything.

> **Q&A** There is a deal struck between baby and parent about what the infant needs to do in order to be loved. In your own life, consider what have been the main things you have done in order to be lovable. Has there been a pattern? Has that pattern worked for you or has it been at considerable personal cost?

Language

A lot of learning requires language. We are designed to take in sequences of sounds and to construct meaning around these. The sequence of sounds converts to a sequence of ideas. We are born knowing a great deal about language, which we use to try to find out what other people do and then we do it too. Our capacity to pick up language is phenomenal.

Young children remember events very well, better than most adults. Despite this most people can rarely remember much from before the age of three.

Some people even dismiss the importance of these years on the basis that 'if it was important I'd remember it!' This is surprising given that some of our most important lessons – how to walk, talk, count, go to the toilet and feel secure – are learned before the age of three.

The reason that we don't remember much before three is that at that time we can't clearly differentiate past thoughts from present thoughts. Babies can't design a continuous autobiographical story about what has happened to them.

From very early on, boys and girls use language differently and this sets up a pattern that can limit their lives and bedevil their relationships. It seems that boys and girls understand the world in dramatically different ways. Unless we question our own views and realise that they may not be the only perspective possible, we can be left puzzled by the actions of the opposite sex.

Broadly speaking, girls are focused on using language to create relationships and connection. Boys are also interested in relationships but use language quite differently to achieve this. They use language to talk about achievements, actions and activities.

It is not only gender that plays a part in our use of language; the order you were born in your family is another influence. Older siblings contribute a lot to younger siblings. Younger brothers or sisters know more about their older siblings than older siblings know about their younger brothers and sisters. If you have older siblings you need to make predictions about them. Just as it's important to know enough to predict others' behaviour, it's important to know about the physical world (for example, it's useful to be able to predict if your brother is about to throw something at you and it's also useful to know how to dodge being hit by it).

Stereotypically, eldest children tend to be bossy, bring the trophies home for their parents' admiration and tell people how to do things; middle children grow big elbows and become attention-seeking trouble-makers; and youngest children lie around looking cute and getting people to do things for them.

The relationships we form with brothers and sisters provide a blueprint for future relationships and are incredibly powerful. They replay throughout our lives. It is through our siblings that we first learn to negotiate to have our needs met. The bonds and the battles re-emerge, as already mentioned, at times of family gathering.

Families send their children off on different missions – one may be the carer, another the entertainer or distracter. This is why, when siblings recall significant family events, they often have markedly different memories. Knowing this can reduce a lot of heat at family gatherings. Your brothers and sisters don't understand your point of view and it's likely they never will.

Children without siblings have the temptation to act like a super-eldest and to become articulate, skilled mini-adults at the cost of losing their childhood prematurely. For them the roles of cousins, friends and school mates will be to smooth off the more glaring edges of pomposity and precosity.

The terrible twos

As terrible two year olds, we do things because our parents don't want us to and through doing so, we learn more about our parents. This is a time of enormous willpower. It is also when we gain an inkling that other people don't exactly see the same things in the way that we do. The revelation that other people may think differently is a source of great curiosity to us. Hide-and-seek games and boundary testing are two of the many ways we use to test this out.

Children develop internalised working models of emotion. For example, if the people they turn to for warmth and comfort turn away when they are distressed, this will influence how they interpret the world; they will see it as not trustworthy and unreliable. Even abused children can escape long-term damage if there is someone who doesn't turn away.

At this time, it is best for us to be in the presence of a positive, loving parent who realises that we are testing him or her and who will gently guide us through these battles.

The way parents view their world sets up a lens through which their children see the world. This is why we need to be very nurturing of new parents. If they are in despair, it is contagious. If parents are joyful, this is also contagious.

Three–four years

At around three to four years of age it all changes. Suddenly what we learned automatically has to be learned through willpower. The way a four-year-old expresses this is to incessantly ask the question, 'Why?'.

At this time many children are mistresses or masters of the universe. They see themselves as magically able to control the world. This means that if bad things happen, children blame themselves for having caused them.

A. A. Milne beautifully stated this in the first stanza of his poem 'Disobedience':

> *James James*
> *Morrison Morrison*
> *Weatherby*
> *George Dupree*
> *Took great*
> *Care of his mother*
> *Though he was only three.*

The early surge of willpower at three to four years can be terrifying to some children. Parents need to demonstrate that they love their children, especially at this time when they are being difficult, in order to create feelings of security. If a three- or four-year-old feels that their tantrum is powerful enough to rule the family home, that can be a scary prospect.

The early whiff of power at this age is also contained in emotion and imagination. Three year olds are immersed in an erotic world. They act like lovers in an Italian opera. They are also terrible liars and are baffled by politeness that pretends one emotion while feeling another. This is a time when their hearts are truly carried on their sleeves.

Four–six years

Between four and six years of age is a delightful time for children raised in a nurturing environment. They assert themselves and their minds are full of schemes, dreams and plans.

Children who are unlucky enough to experience abuse may withdraw into a world of their own. The interior world is, for them, a place of retreat and shadow and children begin to repress material that will haunt them later in their lives. Many of them, still believing they are the masters or mistresses of the universe, may believe they caused the abuse to occur and will be plagued by guilt and shame. Others develop the 'adrenaline brain' that is focused on vigilance and survival rather than learning and happiness. The dreadful experiences they have can spoil them and set them up for a life where compliments and joy fly straight past them.

Just as a small cut on a seedling becomes a major scar in the bark as it grows to be a tree, our early experiences often magnify and echo throughout our lives. Much of our early years is not clearly remembered but obviously that does not mean those years are unimportant. In this time we learn to talk, love, walk, converse, understand how the world works and set ourselves up for the rest of our lives. Even the most shockingly deplorable experiences can be overcome if you are lucky to find someone to care and love you patiently and to help you learn how to play. It takes time to re-build a broken child but no time is better spent.

At 6 years of age:

- Cole Porter starts music lessons.
- Nadia Comaneci is selected to start gymnastics training.
- Mozart begins touring Europe.
- Shirley Temple sings, 'On the Good Ship Lollipop'.
- Ray Charles becomes blind.
- Between 6 and 10, you were eligible to become a vestal virgin – an assistant in the temple of Vesta, Rome.

At 7

- Henry VI has his coronation ceremony.
- In pre-Victorian times you would begin your apprenticeship at 7–12.
- Frederick Chopin publishes his first composition.
- Buster Keaton is already a skilled acrobat.
- The Spartan boy was consigned to the state officer for educating and training.

> **Q&A** To gain a glimpse back into the issues that preoccupied your child mind, see if you can remember the story that you either asked to be read over and over again to you, or that you read to yourself. That you asked for this story to be told repeatedly was not a coincidence. The themes of the story often mirror the issues that perplexed you as a child.

Anyone who has watched a child learn to walk knows you can't learn to walk if you can't learn to fall. You can't learn to love if you can't withstand some rejection. You can't learn to succeed in life unless you can tolerate some setbacks and failures.

Learning to deal with setbacks without shrinking away from them is important. If your parents protect you too much you may learn to avoid the challenges of life. What is avoided in life persists and these challenges plague you for the rest of your life. So children need to be encouraged to face and conquer challenges and to build a life that is broad and rich enough to live in. This is beautifully expressed in one of the teaching parables in Nury Vittachi's *Feng Shui Detective*:

> *It is a hot day. You sit under a very small tree. This is good. There is shade. You can see all around you. Nowhere can hide the interloper.*
>
> *But there is shade. For one person only. You have no visitors. You become lonely.*
>
> *You move to a bigger tree. It has room for two–three guests to share the shade,*
>
> *This is very nice. But the trunk is a bit wide. There is a space behind you. You cannot see who is there. Some of us as we grow older, we move to much larger trees. You find a tree so large that a village can sit in its shade. You have a very*

big world now. But there is danger. Behind you there is an unknown space as big as the space in front of you.

Some people never get to a large tree. Others move from small to big worlds. But something in their lives shocks them. They go back to very small worlds.

When you meet someone you must silently ask them, how big is your world?

This is one of the most important things to know about someone.

In order for children to have a resilient life they need to be encouraged to develop a big world. A world that is rich in experiences so they will develop the skill of wisdom, the ability to flexibly respond to whatever life throws up at them and be able to create a future they can fall in love with.

Childhood
(Ages 8-14)

Childhood is a time of most intense happenings. It is a forest of first encounters. Innocence lets us become aware of what we can handle. Innocence permits the child to belong to the world. This is the secret of the child's trust – the child assumes belonging is natural and warm and sheltering (and ongoing).

As children we are plunged into a world of possibility. Aladdin is a little boy who lives in China and then one day a Sorcerer arrives. Alice is wondering how to amuse herself on a summer's day when a white rabbit vanishes down a mysterious hole. Little Red Riding Hood wanders off into the forest, Hansel and Gretel are abandoned to die in the forest when they meet an apparently kindly old woman, and Jack discovers three beans and ends up battling a giant. A young squire named Arthur removes a sword from a block of stone in St Paul's

> 'Seven years and six months!' Humpty Dumpty repeated thoughtfully. 'An uncomfortable sort of age. Now if you'd asked *my* advice, I'd have said, "Leave off at seven" – but it's too late now.'
> 'I never ask advice about growing,' Alice said indignantly. 'Too proud?' the other enquired. Alice felt even more indignant at this suggestion. 'I mean,' she said, 'that one can't help growing older.' '*One* can't, perhaps,' said Humpty Dumpty, 'but **two** can. With proper assistance, you might have left off at seven.'
> – Alice in Wonderland

Churchyard and becomes King. Harry Potter is living a dismal life as an orphan with his aunt and uncle when an owl arrives with a message which changes his life forever. An obscure shepherd boy called David takes on the giant Philistine, Goliath, and brings him down with a slingshot.

Luke Skywalker is saved by Obi-wan Kenobi and is coached in the ancient ways of the Jedi before battling his father, Darth Vader.

Childhood is a land of possibility and wonder but it is not without its dark side. In fact childhood is scattered with a menacing collection of trolls under bridges, hobgoblins, demons, fire breathing dragons, giants, angry dwarves, poltergeists, monsters under the bed with the odd good fairy thrown in for good measure.

> 'Your children are not your children. They are the sons and daughters of Life's longing for itself.'
> – Kahil Gibran

Childhood experience is infused with wonder. The imagination of children knows no limits. There is a fascination with stories. Children don't just listen to stories, they become them. This is why television, fairytales, and computer games are so powerful.

Children aren't just fascinated with the good in stories. They want the good oil on how to prepare and cope with the evils in life. That is why children are fascinated with stories that feature monsters, boogiemen and sinister goblins.

Good parenting is unselfish and encourages independence in a child. Children are urged to grow and leave the nest.

A child's sensibility is like a sponge. It absorbs everything – the good as well as the bad. We drink in the voices of our parents. All parents leave a trail of imperfection for their children.

While most of us (about 55 per cent) are lucky enough to have parents who help us understand our emotions and can calm and settle us when we are upset, life is not always neat.

There are many reasons why parents do not always create security in their baby's life, such as depression, illness, poverty, stress or their own history of relationships. About 25 per cent of us have early experiences that lead us to not trusting close relationships. During childhood we may become fiercely self-reliant and deny our need at times to be comforted by others. In romantic relationships, the big question becomes 'Can I rely on this person?' As adults we may sabotage or

At 8 years of age:

- Maxim Gorky starts work.
- Shirley Temple receives 135,000 birthday presents in 1936.
- Bjorn Borg starts playing tennis.
- Tiger Woods wins the 9-10-year-old boys' event at the Junior World Golf Championships.

At 9

- Mozart composes his first symphony.
- Marilyn Monroe is taken to Los Angeles Orphans Home where she stays until she is 11.
- Tatum O'Neal stars in *Paper Moon*.
- Jack Nicklaus starts playing golf.

At 10

- Richard II becomes King of England in 1377.
- Jean Piaget writes his first scientific paper.
- Claude Debussy enters the Paris Conservatoire in 1872.
- David Livingstone leaves school.

At 11

- Noel Coward has his first acting engagement.
- W.C. Fields runs away from home.
- Elizabeth Taylor stars in *Lassie Come Home*.
- Billie Jean King saves to buy her first tennis racket.

avoid close relationships. Some of us may turn our energies into our careers or focus all our love onto our children. We are often seen by our lovers and/or partners as cool and aloof.

About 20 per cent of us have early experiences that leave us insecure. Our parents were sometimes tuned in, sometimes not. This leaves us prone to pessimism, clingy or jealous behaviours, dependent on others and with rock bottom self-esteem. We may feel unworthy of being loved and feel mystified that people want to be our friends. We are often incapable of calming or soothing ourselves and rely on others to help us deal with upsets. As adults we start romantic relationships anxiously and worry whether we are worthy of the person we are with. This can lead to panic whenever there is distance or conflict in our romantic lives. Being in love is filled with anxiety but being without love is seen as unbearable.

For most of us, these early experiences resonate throughout our lives and create a mould for all our future relationships.

Mooch time in an ADHD world

Much of childhood today seems to be played indoors and is structured time. Children in the developed world are rushed and overscheduled. Drawing back from the frenzy of life and having some time when nothing is arranged allows for creativity and presence.

Children used to make up games, these days they buy them. Mooch time is important for children. It is a time for unstructured play without electronic entertainment. It is a time when imagination, creativity and concentration can be developed.

Children grow up in a world where Attention Deficit and Hyperactivity Disorder is common. They are over-stimulated, over burdened and de-sensitised. They need time to digest all that is new and learned.

Behaviourally and academically, childhood can be a bumpy ride. There are flare-ups and conflicts. Children need our love most when they deserve it least. By loving them even when they are acting in audacious, outrageous ways we create feelings of security and resilience.

School

In the last generation, success at school has gone from desirable to absolutely vital in many parents' minds. However, basing success solely on academics can be restrictive for many people. There is a strong history of successful people who did poorly at school:

- John Lennon was expelled from kindergarten.
- David Niven was expelled from boarding school (for sending a matchbox full of dog poo to a friend who had pneumonia).
- Gandhi described his schooling as the 'most miserable years of his life'.
- Marcel Proust's teacher considered his compositions disorganised.
- Emile Zola got a zero in literature.
- Winston Churchill, who later won a Nobel Prize for literature, was placed in a remedial English class.

At 12 years of age

- Adolf Hitler attends his first Wagner concert in 1891.
- Edward V becomes King in 1483.
- Mark Twain leaves school
- Jodie Foster stars in the film *Taxi Driver*.
- Horatio Nelson enters the Navy in 1770.

At 13

- Anne Frank is forced into hiding with her family in 1942.
- Michelangelo begins his apprenticeship in 1488.
- Mozart receives a Knighthood of the Order of the Golden Spur from the Pope.
- In ancient Rome the minimum age for marriage was 12 (female) and 14 (male).

At 14

- St Bernadette has visions at Lourdes.
- Adam Smith enters Glasgow University.
- Juliet falls in love with Romeo.
- Cary Grant is expelled from school.
- King Louis XIII of France is married.

- Stephen Crane, Eugene O'Neill, William Faulkner and F. Scott Fitzgerald all failed courses in college.
- Woody Allen said, 'I paid attention to everything but the teachers'.

> 'Seven to eleven is a huge chunk of life, full of dulling and forgetting. It is fabled that we slowly lose the gift of speech with animals, that birds no longer visit our windowsills to converse. As our eyes grow accustomed to sight they armor themselves against wonder.' – Leonard Cohen

During childhood our capabilities, imagination and interests are ignited. If some traits are not activated or encouraged then they may never blossom.

The prevailing wisdom used to be that we inherited a set of genes from our parents that were either expressive or regressive and they dictated the colour of our eyes, the shape of our nose and so on. With the completion of the human genome project that idea was turned on its head. The area of research known as 'epigenetics' has shown that genes have triggers and these are either switched off or on, depending on life experiences. Genetic triggers are not just related to our physical characteristics. They also play a role in the expression of our talents and personality. This means that the old debate of whether it is genetics (or nature) or environment (or nurture) that create the person needs to be updated. It is nature, as it is expressed through nurture.

Given that for many children childhood is an indoor game, there is a risk that certain aspects of their characters may not become activated. This means that the experiences people have during childhood may switch on (or not) particular characteristics. If certain characteristics are not activated they can become part of the unlived life.

The emotional world of childhood

Mid-childhood is a time of great intensity of emotion. It is a time when we have friendships that are very dear to our heart. It is time of bonding, intimacy, crushes, blood brothers or sisters and gangs of friends. The world of childhood friendship is marvellously portrayed in books such as *Swallows and Amazons*, *The Secret Seven*, *The Famous Five* and the *Harry Potter* series.

At around ten years of age, we shift our energy away from others and channel it into creativity, art, poetry, dance. I often think that if I could just take the dreams, fantasies and aspirations of a ten-year-old and preserve them in a jar so that they could be glimpsed from time to time during the turbulence of adolescence, it would be enough to see the adolescent through.

> 'If you think you are too small to make a difference you have obviously never been in bed with a mosquito.'
> – Lauren Burns

> 'So the playground was hell: Chinese burns, pinches, slaps and kicks, and horrible games. I can still hear the noise of a thick wet skipping rope slapping the ground. There'd be a big girl each end and you had to lead through without tripping. Joining in was only marginally less awful than being left out.' – Lorna Sage

Adolescence
(Ages 15-21)

Everything familiar changes. Just as the Incredible Hulk bursts out of his previous shape, during adolescence a new person emerges from the crucible of childhood.

The characters of Romeo and Juliet were aged about fourteen in Shakespeare's play and show the perils of this phase of life well. Breaking away from the dependency of childhood, it is the beginning of a perilous journey.

The teenage years are the time when the membrane separating life experiences from your internal moods and feelings is thinnest. Consciousness of privacy becomes an extreme sport. It is a time when the world seems able to look inside your head and read your most private thoughts while, at the same time, understanding none of them.

It is also a time of powerful projection of thoughts onto other people. Hero worship, idolisation and love swirl around. Passion, desire and lust dominate and titillate.

Adolescence is a time filled with dreams, grief and worries. Few teenagers are able to see any positive qualities in themselves and instead project them onto other people. This is why first love is so powerful.

> 'I had arrived at that difficult and unattractive age of adolescence, conforming to the teenage pattern. I was a worshipper of the foolhardy and the melodramatic, a dreamer and a moper, raging at life and loving it, a mind in a chrysalis yet erupting with sudden bursts of maturing.'
> – Charles Chaplin

Projecting and attributing all of those positive feelings and qualities onto another person is wonderful but it does mean that the adolescent can feel devastated and alone if that fragile first love should not succeed.

The anima, the feminine internal spark, belongs inside yourself and very few people realise this. It is the great message derived from the story of Romeo and Juliet – take care of yourself or lose everything.

Adolescence – a time of grief

Adolescence is a time of grief. You are all at odds and out of sorts. You are alone in a way that you never were during your childhood. It is a time of yearning and longing, heaving and sighing, and feeling that no-one in the world really understands.

If you had a happy childhood, adolescence comes as a bit of a jolt. Part of the loneliness of adolescence is that it's a time when our sense of belonging becomes seriously confused. We no longer relate to our family, our teachers or our siblings in the same way. And the people that we could most obviously relate to – other teenagers – attract and terrify us in equal measure.

All this is why even the most adored child can turn on their parents as a teenager and fiercely spit out, 'You don't love me.' In later life when people grieve they become sad, mournful and teary. The way adolescents grieve is by becoming angry. If there is one thing I have learned from all my years of therapy with adolescents, it is that when I am working with an angry teenager I am talking to a grieving person. I have found this to be a useful way of viewing them compassionately.

For many people the teenage years are a confused, turbulent time. It is a time when rejections are taken to heart, ideals are held high and problems are experienced as catastrophies. It is time when people need to believe in absolute values, absolutely.

During adolescence we shock ourselves. We are so obsessed with who we are now that the pleasant child of just a few months ago could just as well be an alien.

If you ask an adolescent to reflect on how they have

At 15 years of age
- Catherine the Great is married to Peter III.
- Mary Queen of Scots is married.
- Giacomo Casanova loses his virginity to two sisters, Nanetta and Marta.
- Dick Turpin is caught stealing cattle in 1721.

At 16
- Joan of Arc offers her services to the King of France, Charles VII.
- Buddha is married.
- Charles Darwin leaves school.
- Leonardo da Vinci begins his apprenticeship.

At 17
- Henry VIII becomes King in 1509.
- Rodin fails the entrance exam for the Ecole des Beaux-Arts in Paris for the third and last time.
- Alfred Lord Tennyson publishes his first book of poetry.
- Rudyard Kipling is a journalist in India.
- Ernest Hemingway is an ambulance driver in World War I.
- Susan Sontag is married.

changed over the past few years, they often won't be able to clearly answer you. The reason is that they change so much they don't even recognise themselves.

For parents of teenagers this transformation can be completely gobsmacking. Methods of parenting, forms of praise and rewards that worked a treat only a moment ago are no longer effective. While the adolescent is furiously trying to invent him or herself, most parents are scrambling around trying to come to terms with the change.

There is an upsurge of new energy in teenagers and there is a new identity beginning to break through the shell of their childhood. This is a time of heightened awareness. Sexuality looms large. Everything is embarrassing.

> *'I was a fourteen-year-old boy for thirty years.'*
> *— Mickey Rooney*

Gender differences

This awareness is focused differently for teenage girls and boys. Girls want to know, 'do you like or love me?' and are vigilant for shifts in this. Boys, of course, still want to be loved, but even more critical for them is the question, 'Do you respect me?'

If adolescence is a time in which mothers and daughters often talk too much, it is also a time in which fathers and sons talk too little. Many mothers can be too 'up close and personal' at this stage, while too many fathers leave the scene of the battle and go missing in action. Other fathers refuse to modify their parenting methods and either become critical of their children in a misguided mission to improve them or they distance themselves from parenting and become obsolete for a time.

Up until now, parents have become accustomed to having most of their wishes complied with. Their dear child may have objected at the odd moment but generally have always done what the big guy or girl in the family said. To have that sweet child turn, almost overnight, into someone who wants input into the major decisions affecting them is

At 18 years of age

- Schubert completes 189 compositions.
- Lauren Bacall stars with Humphrey Bogart in *To Have or Have Not*.
- Cleopatra becomes joint ruler of Egypt on her marriage to her brother, Ptolemy.
- Tutankhamen dies having been ruler of Egypt since the age of 9.
- Queen Victoria ascends the throne.

At 19

- John Buchan writes a list of books he wants to write.
- Richard Wagner has a symphony performed.
- Toscanini conducts *Aida*.
- Josephine Bakers dances in *La Revue Negre*.
- Buckminster Fuller is expelled from Harvard.

At 20

- Alexander the Great becomes King of Macedonia.
- Lorenzo de Medici becomes ruler of Florence.
- Norma Jean Baker is given a movie contract and a new name – Marilyn Monroe.
- Guglielo Marconi conducts his first experiments with radio transmission in 1894.
- Bob Dylan releases his first album in 1962.

At 21

- Jane Austen writes *Pride and Prejudice*.
- Joan Baez is on the cover of *Time* magazine.
- Lucrezia Borgia marries for the third time.
- Douglas Bader loses both legs in a flying accident.

a shock for parents. Of course teenagers don't have the skills to say, 'Excuse me, would you mind if I make a few suggestions in relation to this decision?' Instead they sneer, demand, rant; in short, they use jackboots where crepe-soled shoes would suffice.

The intense and exhausting war of independence begins at this point in many families. For some, it can leave wounds from which it will take years to recover.

Having a rampaging teenager running rings around his or her parents sends a shiver up the spine of most families. For example, one of the rules of thumb I have always applied in my own therapeutic work is that an angry adolescent almost always equals a depressed mother. The roller coaster of adolescence, one moment demanding freedom the next needing support and someone to depend on, can grind parents down. Sometime it is quicker to help the mother rather than working with the teenager to resolve the anger.

The worst thing you can give an adolescent is everything that they want. Many parents are hell bent on trying to appease and befriend their teenagers. Of course they will fail. It is the job of adolescents and parents to fail one another. It is that perception of 'failure' that causes the emerging teenager to differentiate him or herself from parents.

Boys and girls often battle with parents in different ways and have different agendas. Girls have a rather trickier job than boys. To become 'herself', a girl needs to either reject her mother, or comply and repeat her mother's emotional life. This is why when their child is between fourteen and sixteen many mothers find they can do nothing right in the eyes of their daughter. If the battle to form a separate identity is too harsh, a daughter may reject her own mother and identify solely with her father. This identification can lead women to become driven and relentless in the pursuit of success. If a daughter does not differentiate herself from her mother, she

> 'Adolescence is as brief period of optimism separating a brief period of ignorance from a terminal period of cynicism.'
> – Philip Adams

will often follow in her footsteps. For these daughters, the time that their mother dies is a terrible moment – not only because of the loss but because of the shock and jolt to the daughter's own identity.

To become powerful in their own way girls also must stop seeing their fathers as either protectors or authorities. Fathers who develop adult-to-adult relationships with their daughters provide them with the gifts of individuality and empowerment.

Boys don't have to differentiate themselves from their mothers but they do need to separate their romantic lives from their mother. As Robert Bly puts it, a boy will need to 'steal the key from under the pillow of his sleeping mother'.

> 'Whatever is begun in anger ends in shame.'
> – Benjamin Franklin

The degree of differentiation that a young man makes from his mother is also life determining. If he differentiates himself too much he can become heartless and tough and have problems with intimacy. A man tied too closely to his mother after age eighteen will have difficulty with women in his life. A son who relies on his mother to take care of him often expects the world to excuse him from the business of growing up. He may confuse future female partners with his own mother and expect to be nutured. The resulting disillusionment can often lead to self-sabotage, alcohol, drugs and lengthy unemployment. This is why mothers of sons are often wise enough to say 'I love you and I like you, but I am not going to fuss over you and you cannot rely on me to do everything for you.'

This can be difficult to do because the mother may see her son's battles to differentiate himself from his father as unduly harsh and bloody and be tempted to protect him. The protection comes at a great cost to the son.

The challenge, contest and ritualised aggression that characterises the battles between fathers and their sons at this time often mystifies and upsets mothers. However, boys do need to combat with fathers sufficiently to be respected by them. A son needs to find a way to become a man in his own right to make the transition into manhood.

The repeat of the terrible twos

Fourteen to sixteen years of age is really the terrible twos on a more sophisticated level. It is a demanding time in which there are no half-measures. There is very little that a parent can do right in the eyes of teenagers during this time.

The work of adolescence is to carve a life that is to some extent distinct from their parents, and to form a positive identity. For most people this work is rarely completed before their late twenties.

Parts of adolescents' desires become focused on what to do with their lives. The process of realising your dreams is a fragile and precarious one and makes many teenagers vulnerable to criticism and being crushed.

Ideally, adolescents discover positive attributes to develop an identity from. However, it is not always easy.

One of the saddest sights I know is watching a teenager who has given up on him or herself and believes the future has nothing to offer. For these young people life becomes a problem to be solved rather than a mystery to be uncovered.

If you are anxious it is tempting to form your identity in a negative sense by differentiating yourself from groups that you regard to be 'undesirable'. For example, 'I know who I am because I'm not a goth or emo or nerd or a try-hard.'

While this certainty of identity resolves the anxiety of early adolescence, it can trap people for most of their lives. They can become a narrow cliché of the person that they truly could be. They may become overly conformist or fail to investigate a path of life that is different to the lives their parents have had. They live life as a perpetual adolescent.

Essentially it means that these people don't grow out of adolescence. Some of them will have to wait until their early fifties before they can broaden their lives again.

Adolescence is a fertile mix of dreams, grief, anxieties and disdain for the established world. Limits and rules chafe and are designed to be outwitted.

> *School was all wrong. It didn't teach anybody how to exist from day to day, which was how the poor had to live. School prepared you for life – that thing in the far-off future – but not for the World, the thing you had to face today, tonight, and when you woke up in the morning with no idea of what the new day would bring.*
>
> *When I was a kid there really was no Future. Struggling through one twenty-four was rough enough without brooding about the next one. You could laugh about the Past, because you'd been lucky enough to survive it. But mainly there was only a Present to worry about ...*
>
> *School simply didn't teach you how to be poor and live from day to day. This I had to learn for myself, the best way I could. In the streets I was, according to the present-day standards, a juvenile delinquent. But by the East Side Standards of 1902, I was an honors student.*
>
> Harpo Marx

Schools can be places of incarceration for some teenagers who are impatient to begin forging their way in the world. While the advantages of completing an education are enormous, it is not for everyone.

Here is a list of prominent people who left school early:

- Sir Jack Brabham, racing car driver, 15
- Sir Michael Caine, actor, 16
- Ricky Ponting, cricketer, 15
- Sir Charles Mackerras, musical conductor, 15
- Justice Michael McHugh, High Court judge, 15

- Keran Wicks, founder 400-store Network video chain, 13
- Kathy Lette, author, 15
- Paul Keating, former Prime Minister, 14
- Jodhi Meares, model and fashion designer, 15
- Roger Fletcher, Australia's biggest meat processor, 15
- Bruce Mathieson, Melbourne pokies king, 13
- Lindsay Fox, trucking tycoon, 16
- Tom Potter, Eagle Boys Pizza (Australia's third-largest pizza chain), 15

AT THIS POINT IN HIS CAREER SIMON PAUSED TO REFLECT ON THE TRUE MEANING OF SUCCESS

Aspiring adulthood (Ages 22-28)

Aristotle was the person who decided that twenty-one was the age at which people become adults. These days the process of becoming an adult is quite different and not so many people achieve it before the age of twenty-eight. Some never get beyond adolescence at all. This stage of life has now become an extension of adolescence and is often regarded as the 'terrible twenties'.

Just as realising that the feminine aspects of love and creativity reside within you are important to survive adolescence, getting the right of dose of masculinity is essential in the twenties.

A young man needs to slip out of the warm care and embrace of his mother to become a man in his own right. It helps to have an older wise man as a role model at this time to access the compassion and justice of fully formed masculinity. A young man weak in masculinity remains a mummy's boy and cannot develop his personality properly. He may shirk and avoid the challenges of life and become unmotivated and vulnerable to drugs.

A young woman also needs a balance of inner masculinity or she may destine herself to be irrational, totally body conscious, plagued by anxieties and disorganised. If overridden by masculinity she becomes hard, assertive and domineering. A good relationship with the men in her life sets a young woman up to strike out with positive resolve in the world.

Access to a powerful, sparky adult woman at this time can ignite strengths in a young woman that she doesn't even know are there. Not those nice girls and women who play by the rules, but the wild ones, the erratic ones who sweep in and tinkle the souls of others before leaving to be talked about once they have gone. The pressure to conform and fit in with society means that a young woman can risk highlighting her similarities to others to the extent that she submerges her own uniqueness. An adult woman who has found her own path can inspire a young woman to do the same.

> *The day after graduating from college, I found fifty dollars in the foyer of my Chicago apartment building. The single bill had been folded into eighths and was packed with cocaine. It occurred to me then that if I played my cards right, I might never have to find a job. People lost things all the time. They left class rings on the sinks of public bathrooms and dropped gem-studded earrings at the doors of the opera house. My job was to keep my eyes open and find these things. I didn't want to become one of those coots who combed the beaches of Lake Michigan with a metal detector, but if I paid attention and used my head, I might never have to work again.*

The following afternoon, hung over from cocaine, I found twelve cents and an unopened tin of breath mints. Figuring in my previous fifty dollars, that amounted to twenty-five dollars and six cents per day, which was still a decent wage.

The next morning I discovered two pennies and a comb matted with short curly hairs. The day after that I found a peanut. It was then that I started to worry.

David Sedaris

The lesson of Icarus

As people emerge from the anxieties and stumbling uncertainties of adolescence, the pendulum of their emotions can swing so far that they can feel immortal, powerful and full of opinions and judgements. A good example of this type of experience is the legend of Icarus. Icarus and his inventor father Daedalus escape from the Island of Crete by means of feathered wings. Before they set out, Daedalus gives an impassioned warning to fly neither too high lest the heat of the sun melt the wax holding the wings together, nor too low in case they fall into the sea. Icarus ignores his father's warning believing he knows better, and soars higher and higher before plunging headlong to his death in the sea below.

The art of adulthood is to develop self-confidence without arrogance. The twenties are the time of aspiring adulthood. Please feel free to be offended if you are in this age group! Real adulthood doesn't begin in many parts of the Western world until your twenty-eighth year.

> 'The instinct of nearly all societies is to lock up anybody who is truly free. First, society begins by trying to beat you up. If this fails, they try to poison you. If this fails too, they finish by loading honors on your head.' – Jean Cocteau

At 22 years of age
- Ivan the Great becomes Grand Prince of Moscow.
- Charles Darwin voyages of *The Beagle*.
- Virginia Woolf moves to Bloomsbury in 1904.
- Ernest Hemingway moves to Paris in 1921.
- Harry Houdini first escapes from a hospital straitjacket in 1896.
- Mark Spitz wins seven Olympic gold medals.

At 23
- Isaac Newton watches an apple fall and theorises about gravity in 1666.
- Isabella Beaton publishes the first monthly installment of her Book of Household Management.
- Bonnie Parker is shot to death with her partner Clyde Barrow.

At 24
- At 24 John F. Kennedy enters the Navy in 1941.
- Rod Laver wins six national championships in one season.
- John Travolta stars in *Saturday Night Fever*.

At 25
- Raphael enters the papal court.
- John Donne writes his 'Elegies'.
- Dorothy Parker starts dining at the Algonquin Hotel.
- King Ludwig II of Bavaria starts to build a castle at Neuschwanstein in 1868.

At 26
- Hannibal becomes commander in chief on the Carthaginian forces.
- Albert Einstein publishes five papers in physics.
- Liza Minnelli stars in *Cabaret*.
- John Keats, the poet, dies in a house by the Spanish steps in Rome in 1821.

What used to be completed by your eighteenth birthday now doesn't get done until your twenty-eighth. And that is the work of identity formation.

Getting to know who you are

Identity formation is the process of working out who you are and what you are here for. This may begin during the teenage years but it is only between the ages of twenty-two and twenty-eight that we start to create answers to questions such as:

- Who am I?
- Am I a nerd?
- Am I cool?
- Am I a success?
- Am I a failure?
- Am I popular?
- Am I a social outcast?

There are four main ways that people go through the process of forming an identity.

1. Moratorium

In many ways, this is the healthiest position. It centres around the idea that 'I'm not quite sure who I am, so I'll hang out and wait and see who shows

---

At 27 years of age

- F.W. Woolworth sets up his first store in 1879.
- Captain Matthew Webb becomes the first person to swim the English Channel.
- Hugh Heffner starts *Playboy* magazine.
- Greta Garbo says, 'I want to be alone' in *Grand Hotel*.
- Yuri Gagarin becomes the first human in space.
- Walt Disney invents Mickey Mouse.
- Jerry Jeff Walker writes the song 'Mr Bojangles'.

At 28

- Colonel Gaddafi takes over Libya in 1969.
- Conan Doyle writes his first Sherlock Holmes story.
- Alfred Hitchcock directs his first film, *The Lodger*.
- Michelangelo creates 'David' in Florence.
- Sophocles defeats Aeschylus in the Athens festival drama contest of 468 BC.

> 'Let not young souls be smothered out before they do quaint deeds and fully flaunt their pride. It is the world's one crime its babes grow dull. Its poor are ox-like, limp and leaden eyed. Not that they starve, but starve so dreamlessly, not that they sow but that they seldom reap, not that they serve but they have no gods to serve. Not that they die, but that they die like sheep.' – Vachel Lindsay

up'. This often accompanies contentment and exploration of life for the twenty-something-year-old. All is not so calm in the lives of their parents, however, especially if the young adult decides to remain living at home. Parents find themselves asking, 'Are you planning on taking on paid employment at any stage of your existence? Are you retiring before I've had a chance to?'

Nevertheless, tolerating uncertainty at this time of life pays great dividends. Delaying the decision about the type of person you are and becoming aware of and exploring how life works can set you up for the years ahead. Tolerating ambiguity and confusion about who you are for a time allows you to roam more freely and broadly and explore the wilder shores of life.

2. Achievement

Some young people find a positive identity through being successful. At some stage in their childhood or adolescence, someone said to them, 'You are good at *this*!' Whatever '*this*' is, the child reasons, 'If people think I'm good at *this*, I'll do *this*.' Usually there are lots of rewards for doing '*this*', such as social approval, accolades and love. There is the added benefit of being at the right end of the school hall on speech night.

While this is generally positive, it can also trap people into only doing those activities they were successful at. Without consciously knowing it, these people narrow their lives. They are often the ones who tumble back into my therapy rooms in their late forties or early fifties having climbed the corporate ladder but discovered they had placed it against the wrong wall to begin with.

3. Confusion

Young people remain confused and anxious about who they are. They feel they have no idea of their direction in life and add to the anxiety by feeling they should know by now.

Their fears and worries make them vulnerable to fads, cults, role models (both positive and negative) and, as we will see in the next seven-year stage, work places.

With the compression of childhood that we see in many parts of the world, the worry about not knowing who you are afflicts people younger and younger.

4. Foreclosure

The fourth main way to contend with identity formation is foreclosure. Some young people decide that 'this is all I can be' or 'this is all I can expect from life'. Passions that once burned fiercely, sputter. Dreams are pared back. The shine in their eyes becomes dulled.

Without assistance to alter this position, many of these people suffer deep despair and disappointment about life. Some of them avoid the challenge of entering adulthood and seek a false refuge in drugs. It is important to help people in their twenties to choose love and life rather than drugs. Drugs anesthetise people to life.

Foreclosure is the result of not building a life large enough to encompass your dreams.

> 'If you could see your future laid out for you – that's not your future.'
> – Joseph Campbell

You are more than you know

Just as we need to protect childhood, we need to consolidate adulthood by deepening and understanding ourselves and other people. Self-knowledge at any age is valuable, but acquiring a measure of it in your early twenties is like getting a jump start on having a great life.

You are much, much more than you know. The Johari window (below) provides a good way of understanding the complexity of ourselves. This model suggests that we are all a bit like a four-roomed building.

The four-roomed building has four windows – two you can see into and two only other people can see into. Room 1 is the 'open you'. It is the part of you that other people can see. It is the part of you that is on show. It is the aspect of yourself about which you might say, 'I'm *that* sort of person,' and other people would agree, 'Yes, she's *that* sort of person.'

Room 2 is the private or 'secret you'. This room contains aspects of yourself that you don't readily share. It might be secret information, it might be things you modestly don't share. It is a side of you that very few, if any, people see. You know about these parts but tuck them away from the eyes of others. There is nothing wrong with this.

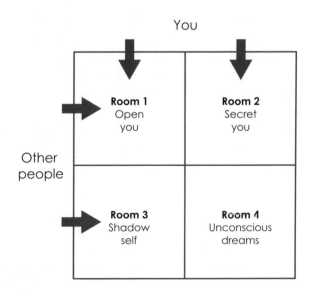

Room 3 contains information about yourself that you don't know about but other people can see. Scary, huh? There are things about you that other people know better than you know. This is known as the 'shadow self'. These are parts of ourselves we keep out of view so well that we just pretend they don't exist.

Room 4 is the part of you that no-one gets to see directly. Not even you. This is your unconscious. A warehouse of information that is usually only accessed through dreams.

Notable psychologist Robert Johnson defines dreams as things your unconscious mind knows that you don't. Dreams are like your unconscious mind hammering on the door of your conscious mind and yelling, 'Hey! Wake up! You need to know this!' Dreams contain important knowledge that, if we take the time to reflect on them, often provide valuable information. Dreams unfortunately don't speak adult. Instead they speak in the language of images, symbols and childhood. As such, it takes some effort to unravel their meanings.

For people interested in this area, the first thing to do is to notice and record your dreams. Keep a pad and pen by your bed and write down anything you can recall of the dream before you get up. Put as much detail in as you possibly can. People who say 'I never dream' often find that doing this means they begin to remember fragments of their dreams for the first time.

The second thing is to remain curious about the dream. It is very common for people to dismiss dreams saying something like, 'I had a weird dream last night that makes no sense at all,' and to think no more about it.

The next thing is to talk to someone about the dream. Find someone who is prepared to reflect and consider what it might be saying. They probably won't understand the dream either. Nevertheless, their questions, perspectives and thoughts about your dream will help you to crystallise your own understanding.

One of the principles about analysing a dream is that it is all about you. Every part of the dream represents a part of you. So if you dream about your aunty or your friend, it is not particularly helpful to ask yourself what that tells you about your aunty or friend. Instead it is much more useful to ask yourself, 'What does that tell me about the part of myself that *is like* my aunty or my friend?'

A very simple example might be if you dreamed about a friend of yours (who you considered to be a successful but driven soul) riding upwards in a lift. A question you might ask yourself would be, 'Is the ambitious part of me that is similar to my friend trying to scale the lofty heights too quickly?'

Dreams rarely provide answers but they do provide useful perspectives, viewpoints and questions for you to consider. To continue our simplified example of the lift dream, a consideration would be, 'Should I slow down a bit and trust that I will succeed at my own rate?'

This book has a big enough task trying to cover human life without adding dream analysis to its contents. Therefore, a comprehensive coverage of dream analysis will not be attempted. Nevertheless, here are a few practical points.

1. Machines in dreams are usually bad news. They usually indicate that the person is working too hard, moving too fast or making a mistake.
2. Dreams about physical illnesses are important. If you dream that you have something physically wrong with you, get it properly checked out. Don't delay. Sometimes we know something is physically wrong at an unconscious level before we become fully aware of it.

The final thing is to ask yourself, 'What do I do with this information from the dream?' Of course you don't *have* to do anything. It often seems sufficient to symbolically acknowledge the message of the dream. To continue our simplified example, the dreamer having recognised that he or she is scaling the heights of work and success doesn't need to give it all up and retreat to a beach for a year. Instead, scheduling in some time off or being aware of the signs of overload may be enough.

Learning about the complexity of yourself in your twenties is a massive advantage. By being aware of the different sides to your identity, you allow yourself to encounter all sorts of different life experiences, widening your perspective and gaining valuable knowledge from unexpected sources. The more colours you have on your palette, the more vivid your canvas will be. The open you, the hidden you, the part of you that you are unaware of, and the unconscious you, all play a role in your life.

The twenties is a try-out time, during which we identify with different groups, often co-habit with odd-bods and try out different types of values, relationships, lifestyles and jobs.

> 'There is a vitality, a life force, a quickening that is translated through you into action, and because there is only one of you in all time, this expression is unique. And if you block it, it will never exist through any other medium and be lost. The world will not have it. It is not your business to determine how good it is, nor how valuable it is, nor how it compares with other expressions. It is your business to keep it yours clearly and directly, to keep the channel open. You do not even have to believe in yourself or your work. You have to keep yourself open and aware directly to the urges that motivate you. Keep the channel open.' – Martha Graham, dancer and choreographer

Growing an even bigger world

The twenties can be one of the most dynamic and formative periods in life. For many it is just that – a time to flourish away from the protective eyes of parents. The experimentation that is undertaken during this phase determines the way in which subsequent adult values form.

Unfortunately for some the challenge of life seems all too daunting. Obviously this is not new, Benjamin Franklin once remarked that many people die at twenty-five but they are not buried until they are seventy-five.

The twenties is a time for rites of passage. It is a time to be adventurous and to learn about life. If you do not get enough life experience at this time it can be tricky to find out what you really feel passionate about.

One danger of the twenties is to become so comfortable with your life that you begin to believe it will go on like this forever. This can lead to a premature rush towards feelings of belonging and safety. Some of the people who follow this path can become intolerant and judgemental of others who find life more challenging. It is almost as if their own level of comfort blinds them to the vagaries of life for others. There will be shocks in store. Life is difficult and belonging has to change if we are to continue to grow.

As the poet David Whyte notes, life has a way of disrupting your sense of belonging. At the very moment when the home fire is crackling and a glass of something good is in hand and you are sighing with deep contentment to have found the place where you should be, there is a tap on the door and you are turfed out.

In our twenties, we are constantly re-adjusting to a new identity. The key questions at this stage of life are:

- What am I here for?
- What type of work will I do?
- Who will I be in a relationship with?
- What is success for me and how will I find it?

Breaking out of your own cocoon

We no longer prepare people well for adulthood. There is an apocryphal story that relates to this. A man discovers a cocoon and decides to watch closely the caterpillar struggling to break out of its shell to become a butterfly. After a while, the man realises he hasn't got all day to watch this process and decides to lend the struggling caterpillar a helping hand by gently prising the cocoon open. The butterfly emerges but it is stunted and unable to fly. The struggle of breaking open the cocoon is what gives the fledgling butterfly's wings the strength it needs to fly.

Like the caterpillar, to struggle is important. It forges our character. Just as the trees grow strongest where they are buffeted by winds, we also need challenges and obstacles in life in order to learn how to become strong and resilient.

If you are lucky, around the age of twenty-four, you learn that people are generally happiest and healthiest when their lives are expanding rather than contracting. Accompanying this discovery is defiance: twenty-four year olds often say they will never do what their parents did, then do precisely what their parents did. The model of relationships witnessed as children act like templates that we use to assess all of our future relationships. It takes a great deal of thought, courage and awareness of who we are to break the mould of previous generations and create a new way of relating to others.

This is why having a mentor at this age is a wonderful thing. Ideally, it should be someone ten–fifteen years older who has a good sense of who they are and what is required to make your way in the world.

If you could choose three mentors that you know personally who would you choose? If you could have three mentors from any time in history who would you choose?

Without some kind and gentle mentoring, aspiring adults can make the most awful blunders. Many result in lost romantic relationships, job loss and rejection. The positive and aspirational achievement-driven young adults are just as prone to making catastrophic mistakes as those in foreclosure.

Young people can be too blunt, too competitive or too erratic under stress and use their growing power in unwise ways. The world is unforgiving to aspiring adults who make such mistakes. Of course, these mistakes may also be viewed as essential blunders, and provide some of the most valuable lessons of life.

The temptation for parents to try and protect their young adults from setbacks is perilous. Providing their children with economic outpatient care can lead to the loss of emerging adult status. Prolonging dependency results in arrested emotional development and an inability to gain access into the adult world.

When setbacks occur, and we can be sure that they will, fantasies of death are quite common. Many twenty-two year olds don't think they will live beyond thirty. The failure of many prominent and not-so-prominent people to survive to their thirtieth birthday is remarkable.

Twenties Death toll
Buddy Holly, 22
Duane Allman, 24
Brian Jones (Rolling Stones), 25
Janis Joplin, 27
Jimi Hendrix, 27
Jim Morrison, 27
Heath Ledger, 28
Marc Bolan, 29

Part of our struggle as young adults is to refine the direction of our life and retain some of the idealism of adolescence. Keith Richards once said that you think you should shoot yourself when you reach thirty, then when you get there, you put away the gun.

Creating belonging as an adult

Responding to adversity requires people to flexibly call upon internal and external resources. Androgyny, the ability to use the masculine and feminine sides of yourself, has a powerful role in developing feelings of resilience and belonging.

When a man loses touch with his feminine side (the anima) he becomes lonely, moody and driven to compete. Hard-edged and task oriented, he experiences a bankruptcy of spirit and belonging and is well on his way to becoming a glowing success story with heart problems and troubled relationships. Most of his actions are directed at satisfying the glory of his own ego. His main sense of belonging will come from the latest victory over his rivals. The whiff of success is intoxicating but brief, and it is usually followed by a deflated ego and discontent which is disregarded as he presses on to the next victory.

If we think of belonging as consisting of two impulses: being and longing, we can consider the impulse of longing to be associated with the masculine (the animus) and the sense of being more strongly associated with the feminine (the anima) within us.

Society devotes so much time to the masculine sense of longing that it neglects the power of the feminine. All too often we value science over the humanities, specialisation over integration, the mechanical over the emotional, achievement over collaboration, the short-term gain over the sustainable, action over consideration, fragmentation over coherence, problem solving over problem sharing and individualism over community.

This is not to say that all masculine impulses are misguided. Indeed, many of the great gains of public welfare and health have been achieved through the masculine drive. As Camille Paglia, the feminist writer, once dryly commented, if it were entirely left to the feminine we would all still be living in grass houses.

However, a world imbalanced in its values, not only risks an epidemic of meaninglessness, it also loses the vital combination of forces that allow it to change things for the better, and to flourish.

In a similar way, a woman who has distorted contact with her masculine side either loses a sense of her own power to create change in the world or becomes tyrannically angry.

I see increasing numbers of angry young women in my therapy room. Often they are angry that life and their mothers have let them down. Now I like to see young women being feisty but this is different. These young women are furious but ineffectual and their anger is all too often turned inwards on themselves in the form of eating disorders or self-harm. Some of these young women turn themselves into victims but it is they who most suffer the consequences.

Alternatively, a young woman may only value herself as an object to be sexually desired, deciding that it is more important to be desired by others than to have desires herself. She may become vulnerable to society's stereotype of women as either shag, hag, nag, witch or bitch. (The male equivalent for this has to be yob, slob, knob, sleaze or squeeze!)

She may also take on the role of a martyr and enact pathetic servitude. Many of you will know adult women who take on this role. In some countries this is known as the burnt chop syndrome, as in 'Don't worry, dear, I'll have the burnt chop.'

It seems to me that men often get into a muddle in relation to their feminine side. They also regularly confuse their inner feminine aspects (anima) with real flesh and blood women. The very spark they idolise in someone else is the same spark that they deny having themselves.

Falling in love – twenties style

One of the great tragedies of the modern world is that both men and women take their own anima – their internalised feminine selves, their spark – and project it onto other people. I see many people in their twenties who fall head over heels in love and ascribe all that is positive and wonderful in their lives to their partner. As wonderful as that person no doubt is, they fail to appreciate what is divine about themselves and in doing so place themselves at risk. For if you rely on someone else to provide the wonder of life, you may stunt your own growth.

We fail to differentiate *loving* someone from being *in love* with someone. When we fall in love we ask someone to undertake something angelic for us. We ask someone to release or make visible 'the angels' that reside within us all. Falling in love is so magnificent because not only do we get to see the beauty of someone else at this time, we get a chance to glimpse the very best of ourselves. Ideally, falling in love transforms your life and you use it to build a better, stronger person.

But if you do not, if you continue to project your anima onto a flesh and blood person, no living person can live up to this projection and eventually it wears thin. Some men, when they find the initial flames of passion

> '… give up what needs to be given up, prune what has to be pruned, strive without embarrassment or apology to be virtuous, be discerning, choose wisely, struggle; and eventually you will surely find the means you need to live each day in the way you were meant to live it, and to become the person you were meant to be.
> Herein lies the ultimate struggle of mind and heart. It is a choice that we can make, and it is the only choice that matters. And that choice is ours.' – Harry Moody and David Carroll

cooling, fail to take on board the lessons and instead rush off to fall in love with someone else. Seemingly they do this in seven-year cycles. Women are also prone to do this.

Some people establish relationships early on in life and keep them going successfully. Others find that an early romantic relationship may fall apart in their later twenties as their expectations of life begin to shift.

Creating lives that count

Particularly around the age of twenty-seven, you often experience an event that completely throws you. It may be a job change, the end of studies or a relationship change. At this time you can either rush back into your parents' embrace, bind yourself to a romantic partner or learn how to parent your self. This time is often accompanied by a first taste of conservatism and cautiousness.

During the twenties you need to let enough people catch your eye so that some of them can catch your heart. Once your heart has been caught the job is then to keep it open. You must remember to incorporate anima, vitality and creativity into your life, value both the masculine and the feminine in yourself, and parent and care for yourself.

The great fear is that we lose the path of life and find ourselves barren with nowhere to belong. As Dante's 'Comedia' teaches us, emptiness is not a place we can live but if we want freedom it is a place we must at some stage of our lives pass through.

As mentioned previously, the great message from *Romeo and Juliet* is take care of yourself or lose everything. When we neglect what matters to us that becomes the matter with us. We want to not just create lives that work but live lives that count.

22–28 Aspiring adulthood

Do:
- Extend friendships with both men and women.
- Travel and have adventures.
- Realise that your behaviour at school and the marks you received will no longer suffice in the real world.
- Begin the process of understanding yourself – talk to people you trust, who will nourish your dreams, ideas and aspirations without belittling or mocking them.
- Let parents, family, brothers and sisters as well as friends comfort you. As you move from your family into the world there will be times of loneliness.
- Gain a wide range of work experiences.
- Boldly try out new activities. Explore life as widely and as richly as you can.
- Develop your skills: analyse what you are good at and do it.

Avoid:
- Being tamed too early.
- Letting your fears back you into a corner in life. If a relationship, course or job is not for you, be prepared to change.
- Allowing your romances to cause you to neglect your friendships.
- Being too stretched as you try out a wide range of things.
- Using alcohol or drugs to build your confidence in social situations.

Prepare for:
- Vibrancy.
- Further education.

Read:
- *The Inner Game of Tennis: The Classic Guide to the Mental Side of Peak Performance* by Timothy Gallway.
- *If You Meet Buddha on the Road, Kill Him!* by Sheldon Kopp.
- *Strengths Finder* by Tom Rath.
- *What Colour Is My Parachute?* by Richard Bolles.
- *Wishcraft: How to Get What You Really Want* by Barbara Sher.

The Napoleon years (Ages 29-35)

The twenty-ninth year should begin with theme music: the twang of the umbilical cord finally snapping. These are the Napoleon years. A time when you think you can make a plan and it might just come off!

This is a time of great endeavour, energy and enterprise. With clear headedness we can achieve a lot during these years, accomplishments that will set us up for the rest of our lives. It is a time to use our strengths and to tame, or at least know, our shortcomings.

The Napoleon years are when the flaws in our character can endanger us. If left unchecked, the certainty we may feel at this time can lead to reckless arrogance. There are flaws in us all and they show up vividly during these years. The Greeks described these flaws as hubris, or over-weaning pride. ('Nothing in excess' was inscribed over the temple of Apollo in Delphi.)

Greek tragedies show heroes who, though noble in character, have fatal flaws which catch them out, leading to their destruction. This has been explored extensively throughout our history and literature. Samson admits the source of his power (his hair) and loses his strength. Shakespeare's King Lear insists on declarations of love and loses Cordelia, the daughter who truly loves him. Robinson Crusoe is a spirited adventurer but is also feckless, aimless, and all at sea. In Coleridge's 'The Rime of the Ancient Mariner' the limited awareness of the seaman leads him to kill the albatross (a symbol of wholeness).

During this stage of life we need to temper our recklessness with consideration for others and for ourselves. Without this consideration, our flaws can become inflated and dominate our lives. If they become too pronounced, as Robbie Burns the beautiful Scottish poet put it well, 'The best laid schemes of mice and men. Will go astray.'

The essential flaws in us all

We are all flawed. However, it may be that our flaws are the most passionate and loveable parts of ourselves. Many of us carry around a delusion that if we perfected ourselves just a little bit more, by losing that weight, hiding those wrinkles or laughing less raucously, we would be more loveable. In truth it is our idiosyncrasies and flaws that are loved.

The flaws that we often see in ourselves rarely match the flaws others see in us. We can strive to conceal flaws but they have a way of showing themselves. All we can do is to try to practise loving acceptance of ourselves – flaws and all.

'Show me a hero and I'll write you a tragedy.' – F. Scott Fitzgerald

If you go to a funeral you will often hear about the accomplishments of the recently deceased person, but what always touches the hearts of others are the stories of that person's quirks, passions and, if told lovingly, their limitations. It is our tiny moments of madness that make us bearable and loveable.

I once heard a wonderful story about Mozart. He wrote a symphony so structurally perfect, so beautifully balanced that it was boring. Mozart decided to improve it by putting in some notes that were too long and others that were slightly imperfect to give the piece liveliness and richness.

The problem is not that we are flawed. We all are. The problem is that we fail to look within, and develop a mindfulness of our interior world.

> *Neither look forward where there is doubt, nor backwards where there is regret. Look inward and ask not if there is anything outside that you want, but whether there is anything inside that you have not yet unpacked.*
>
> Quentin Crisp

The departure of your Guardian Angel

There is an old proverb that your guardian angel looks after you till twenty-eight, then you're on your own. This is the time when people believe they can set up a plan and it will succeed, and it does – for a while.

Physically we are strong at this age, and for many people this is the first time that they truly take on the challenge of life. It is the 'little engine that could' time – 'I think I can, I think I can!' Not so long ago this was the time when many people would begin having and raising children.

Today that is often delayed as they bind themselves to jobs. The increasing fickleness of corporate loyalty to employees has, sadly, resulted in more distrust but more devotion. People in this age group are especially distrustful of social institutions, but also devote inordinate hours to their workplace in a type of battle to be the chosen one – employee of the month.

At the very moment that many people are capable of becoming an adult they are catapulted back into an organisational re-run of the rivalry they had with their brothers and sisters. They compete with fellow employees of a similar age vying for the acceptance of a boss. People surrender their own freedom, especially in the workplace, in return for protection and promotion.

> 'Anyone who thinks money can't buy happiness is shopping in the wrong places.'
> – Malcolm Forbes

This is the age of vulnerability where systems such as workplaces have an incredibly invasive grip on people because they can offer a kind of security and belonging. Some people devote their lives and their dreams to workplaces – only to have these progressively crushed.

How love can kill you

While the giddy light headedness of teen love is captivating, it is in the Napoleon years that love gains a much sharper focus. The late twenties and early thirties appear to be a head-long rush to find Mr or Ms Right. With the biological clock ticking ever louder, the rush towards pairing up in the Napoleon years becomes increasingly frenzied.

I see many young women in this age range who find a partner only to sabotage their relationships through premature domestication. The baby's booties are being knitted before the lingerie has been fully appreciated. Of course, this gives many men the heebie-jeebies and they flee. Men at any age, but especially this one, want both love and freedom.

We live in a world that is impoverished in its vocabulary. The Persians had fifty-two words describing different types of love; we, of course, have one. By focusing only on the romantic forms of desire and love, we lose the ability to look within ourselves for nourishment, energy and solace. We risk being dependent emotionally on others, focused on the external and not fully formed as people.

If you are not enabled to fully form as a person you not only struggle to live out the life that is truly yours, you can form relationships with others where differences become threatening. So you settle down into a prison of the mediocre; placing limits and barriers on each other that give the illusion of security and fidelity but stop you from thriving and keep you merely surviving.

> 'Love one another, but make not a bond of love... the oak tree and the cypress grow not in each other's shadow'
> – Kahil Gibran

Too many people do not learn to take responsibility for integrating their masculine and feminine aspects and bring only a partially formed self into their relationships, expecting their partners to make up for the deficiencies in themselves. Partners, wives, husbands, boyfriends and girlfriends are rarely able to remedy flaws in each other. At best they can compensate and make do.

For example, I see some wonderful couples in therapy; sweet people, lovely people who fell head-over-heels in love at school and were too polite and too damn nice, to ever break up the relationship. Perhaps it was fear of loneliness, of not finding someone else, or perhaps they were each just being too kind to the other and not kind enough to themselves. But by their thirties and forties they have not developed as individuals, they confused being close with being compatible and they live in relationships that bore and stifle them.

Society's obsession with romantic love distracts people from learning how to love themselves. For younger people this means that when their first treasured love falls apart – when a romantic love ends – they are devastated and alone in a way that makes them despair.

At 29 years of age:

- Buddha leaves his wife and newborn son.
- James Watt discovers the design for the steam engine.
- Jack Kerouac writes *On The Road*.
- Emily Brontë publishes *Wuthering Heights*.
- Agatha Christie publishes her first mystery.

At 30

- You are old enough to become a Bishop in the Anglican Church.
- Thomas Edison invents the phonograph in 1877.
- Al Capone is involved in the St Valentine's Day Massacre in 1929.
- Lawrence of Arabia enters Damascus.
- Mozart writes *The Marriage of Figaro*.

At 31

- Germaine Greer writes *The Female Eunuch*.

At 32

- Beethoven establishes himself as a composer.

At 33

- Michelangelo begins work on the Sistine Chapel.
- Eva Peron dies in 1952.
- Winston Churchill receives his first Cabinet post.
- Marilyn Munroe stars in *Some Like it Hot*.

At 35

- John F. Kennedy is elected to the Senate.
- Guy Fawkes tries to blow up Parliament.
- Buddha becomes enlightened.
- Tolstoy begins *War and Peace*.
- Louisa Alcott writes *Little Women*.

They risk finding life not worth living, or rush headlong into the arms of another to soothe the wound of their loneliness.

Some younger men are especially vulnerable in this way. By falling in love they have had the opportunity to glimpse for the first time their inner feminine selves. Some men live lives of such action and impact that they spend little time reflecting on their own inner selves. It is often through love that they get to glimpse a powerful mix of strength, willpower and sensitivity within themselves. Until then they quite often have no knowledge of the beautiful person that is within them.

The point here is that to be truly loving and compassionate to others, people first need to love and be good to themselves. They need to attend to their internal world and to find ways of integrating their powers for action and strength (masculine) with the capacity for emotion, imagination and play (feminine). They need to develop an enthusiasm for themselves. Incidentally, the word 'enthusiasm' comes from the Greek '*en theos*' meaning the God within.

Am I really successful?

The Napoleon years are the first review point in many people's lives, a brief pause for introspection and evaluation. This is when the desire to grow up can become a yearning to grow down. One woman described it as feeling shirty, dirty and thirty!

For many people the definition of success alters greatly between the ages of twenty-nine and thirty-three. This can be a perplexing time for many women. 'Do I go for babies, career or both? Do I wear a cape, put my underwear on the outside and try to avoid the kryptonite?' The decision a woman makes about whether to battle it out in the masculine jungle of individual achievement or start mothering will determine the rest of her days.

As we move toward the mid-thirties the sense of urgency gears up for men as well as women. 'If I don't make it by my thirty-fifth birthday I won't make it at all,' seems to be the fear. This can be a perilous idea. Men are very concerned about their ability to provide for their families and be successful by thirty-five. For some women the focus is on careers and achieving financial security by thirty-five, for others it is relationships and babies.

Men and women in their early thirties often seem to be miles apart without realising it. Many of the men I meet recognise that women are largely incomprehensible to them. Many of the women I meet think they understand the men in their lives and are then shocked when they find out they do not.

> 'Obstacles are those frightful things you see when you take your eyes off your goal.'
> — Henry Ford

Nevertheless, it is women who may be most able to cope with the changes that life demands at this time. Some women have already been acutely acquainted with the cyclic naure of life through menstruation, pregnancy and/or miscarriage or abortion. The grief of miscarriage and abortion is often dismissed by the larger world, which can cause a sense of being misunderstood and feeling hurt or angry.

Launching hand grenades into relationships

For a woman who becomes a mother during this time, the experience alters her completely. Sigmund Freud maintained that new mothers are in a symbiotic entanglement with their newborn child. They are undifferentiated from one another. The closed world of mother and child supports both. The child is adored and nurtured. For the new mother it is often a time to re-mother herself.

Alternatively it can be a time when the deprivations and abandonment of her own early life revisits her as depression. This is especially the case if the baby's father is unavailable or is caught up in the demands of providing for the family.

The addition of a baby to a new couple is like launching a grenade into their lives. When the dust and debris settle, nothing will ever be the same.

At this time, the definitions of success for many men and women are poles apart. For women, success is often achieved through connectedness and relationships; for men it is through accomplishment. Both pathways are viable and both have their costs and consequences.

The dreams and desires of men and women can become distorted under the stresses of early family life and flicker into conflict and feelings of hurt. If this pattern is allowed to twist itself into bitterness and contempt, intimacy is in peril and accusations and pain can be traded back and forth. It is important to help new parents hold onto their dreams.

Some men immerse themselves in fathering at this time and experience a wonderful chance to play and nurture. The participation of new fathers in the feminine world of nappies and finger painting is often viewed dismissively by the crusty warhorses of masculinity. However, some older men speak with delight of this experience having achieved it either through a second family or grandchildren. If a man is distanced from his own biological family, becoming a father is often associated with a power surge of connection, belonging, joy and security.

Some women take a supportive role for the men in their lives at this time. They subvert their own creativity and skills in order to bolster their male partner who they perceive to be more talented. However, in a world dominated by masculine impulses, the decision to relinquish your own talents to support someone else is viewed derisively. You may be seen as, and come to see yourself as dull, with little to say.

Some men experience parenthood as merely a blip on the monitor of life and barely draw breath. If they puzzle over their female partner's new intensity and preoccupation, it is fleetingly. Many such men are still flailing around with the sabre and lance making good on the

> 'I'd like to go on being thirty-five for a long time.'
> – Margaret Thatcher, 1979

battlefield of individual achievement. The man they see in the mirror in the morning is just the same, they think. The derring-do adventures of boyhood have been replaced by equally thrilling jousts in the workplace. They are making their way in the world. The Peter Pan they see is just the same as ever. Life hasn't changed a bit, has it?

29–35 The Napoleon years

Do:
- Focus on developing talents, skills and experiences.
- Become a leader of your life – don't wait for others to create possibilities for you or for the situation to be right.
- Foster daring.
- Deepen and preserve friendships.
- Collaborate – in a time of life when competitiveness can predominate, stand out by being a collaborator.
- Nurture your relationships with your extended family.
- Maximise your ability to love well.
- Read stories of inspirational leaders.

Avoid:
- Giving up your wild ways too early.
- Comparisons with others. Envy, jealousy and feelings of failure can beset people.
- Thinking that what is right for you now is right for other people.

Prepare for:
- Changes in your priorities and relationships with others.

Read:
- *Flow: The psychology of happiness* by M. Csikszentmihalyi.
- *Mediation and Relaxation in Plain English* by Bob Sharples.

Clinging to the wreckage (Age 36-42)

Announcing a new diagnostic category – ADULT! The age of 36–42 is frequently a powerful time for people. As Oscar Wilde said, 'From here on down, it's uphill all the way.' From twenty-nine to thirty-five we try ourselves out in various adult roles. But from the age of thirty-six adulthood is the real deal. No longer can we dive under the sheets and claim inexperience or innocence as a defence.

This is a time of immense willpower. Around the age of thirty-six in particular there is often a burst of energy leading to expansion, intellectual growth and optimism. People often take on new ventures, promotions, businesses and endeavours at this time.

If you are lucky enough to have kept a friendship group intact from school or tertiary education days, it is now that the group falls apart, often in dramatic circumstances. The drama is usually based on the theme of, 'You slept with who?'

For those who haven't risen to the challenges of life up until this point, there is an interesting role model that we see in some Western movies and stories: the outsider who rides into town and makes a contribution before hitting the road again. The role of the wanderer is someone who has placed longing over belonging and who has travelled too long to ever settle anywhere or with anyone. Some drifters in our world are, of course, happily building up frequent flyer points in relationships, as well as with airlines.

> 'Middle Age is always ten years older than you are.'
> – Jack Benny

Success is often accompanied by the seeds of discontent at this time: 'Is this really what I want to be doing?' At thirty-six there is a chance to review core beliefs, an opportunity to expand your horizons and feel empowered about your future. Here is a traditional Chinese fable that perfectly captures the conflicting feelings of success and discontent you may feel in your late thirties:

Once upon a time there was a stonecutter. Every day he travelled to work and back again. He was very happy. One evening on his way home he passed the richest man's house in the village and looked in the window. Peering through the window he could see beautiful chandeliers and soft couches and the richest brocades. 'Ah, I wish I was the richest man in the village,' sighed the stonecutter. And an angel came and said, 'So be the richest man.' And he was. He lived in the finest situation and ate the most expensive foods and slept on the sweetest mattress you could find. He was very happy.

And then one day a prince passed by in a golden carriage with a canopy over his head drawn by four beautiful white horses. 'Ah, I wish I was the Prince,' sighed the stonecutter. And an angel came and said, 'So be the Prince.' And he was. He rode around in his carriage and lived the finest of lives. He was very happy.

And then one day he looked up and felt the sun's rays beating on his head. And he said, ' That sun is more powerful than me, I wish I were the sun.' And an angel came and said, 'So be the sun.' And so he was. And he beamed down upon the world and he was very happy and very powerful. He was so powerful he made the crops fail and rivers dry up. He was very strong and very, very happy.

And then one day he looked down and saw a cloud blocking his rays from the earth and he said, 'That cloud is more powerful than me, I wish I were the cloud.' And an angel came and said, 'So be the cloud.' And he was. He blocked the sun's rays and made the earth dark and bleak. The crops again failed and floods spread across the earth. He was very powerful, very strong and very, very happy.

And then one day, a strong wind came and blew the cloud away. 'That wind,' he cried, 'is more powerful than me. I wish I were the wind.' And an angel came and said, 'So be the wind.' And so he was and he blew across the world. Everything was shaken with his power.

Everything except for a cliff. It stood strong and resolute in the face of the wind. 'That cliff is more powerful than I am,' he said. 'I wish I were the wind.' And an angel came and said, 'So be the cliff.' And he was. He felt very, very strong and very, very powerful and he was happy.

And then one day, as the cliff, he felt a tickling at his feet. A stonecutter was slowly but surely chipping him away ...

What is your real legacy?

For people who are parents there is an important question to be answered at this time: What is your real legacy? Is it the money you will leave your children when you are dead or the time that you spend with them while you are alive?

Between thirty-seven and forty-two, many people find a new self-image. This can be a time of stability and contentment. It can be a richly rewarding time if you acknowledge that following a path of personal integrity and honesty is as important as following a career path.

Women are not allowed to age naturally in our society and the stresses on new mothers are enormous. Raising children in isolation can be an incredible burden. New mothers have to contend with child-rearing, weariness, loss of figure, lack of fitness and changes to romantic and sexual relationships. Often the delight of a new baby is followed by social ostracism and loneliness as men devote time to work. In the Western world the 'baby blues' are a very common experience for new mothers.

> 'Never trust a woman who wears mauve, whatever her age may be, or a woman over thirty-five who is fond of pink ribbons, It always means they have a history.'
> — Oscar Wilde

Women who have not experienced pregnancy may have dominant animus (the inner masculine) and may resemble men in the competitive cutthroat workplace. Many women, of course, achieve a balance by directing energies into loving and caring for pets or extended family members.

Women tend to mature during pregnancy. There can be a loss of the playful capering quality of girlhood and a tendency to become a serious protector of their brood. The fear of losing an infant may be, for some women, their first thoughts of death. Nightmares of attacks to the child may haunt her sleep. Others who have experienced miscarriage or abortion previously may be preoccupied by anxieties and dangers to their child.

Men at this time are often thrashing around trying to get a grip on life. Many men who are fathers take on promotions and work longer hours and, in essence, sacrifice themselves for the financial betterment of their families.

Some men use these years to prove themselves to their own fathers. Great frustrations can exist between sons of this age and the perceived expectations of their fathers. In my work with men of this age, I suggest that they spend time together physically with their fathers but when they are away from them to pretend that they are dead.

> 'The Gross National Product does not allow for the health of our children, the quality of their education, or the joy of their play. It does not include the beauty of our poetry or the strength of our marriages; the intelligence of our public debate or the integrity of our public officials. It measures neither our wit or our courage; neither our wisdom nor our learning; neither our compassion nor our devotion to our country; it measures everything, in short, except that which makes life worthwhile.'
> – Robert Kennedy (41)

The power and omnipotence of this time of life can cause some people to unintentionally treat their families as walk-on extras in their latest career dramas. While they bustle around filled with self-importance, life has a way of unravelling. One of the great themes of comedy is people thinking they have it all under their control while in reality it is all going belly-up. Some examples include Basil Fawlty chaotically running his hotel in Torquay; Bertie Wooster being continually saved and controlled by the imperturbable Jeeves; Jim Hacker and Sir Humphrey Appleby's machinations and manoeuvres in

> 'You cannot prevent the birds of sorrow from flying over your head but you can prevent them from building nests in your hair.'
> – Chinese proverb

Yes Minister and most of the *Laurel and Hardy* films show ego out of control.

Women are perhaps less vulnerable to the puffed-up busyness of the ego, but not always. Many mothers reduce their working hours, decline promotions and gain fulfilment through raising children. Other women believe the super-woman myth that they can have it all. Delaying motherhood and donning the battle gear of the corporate world, can lead to some women becoming super–feminists. They may feel successful but at the same time feel out-of-synch with themselves.

At social gatherings there can be a sharp division of women into the 'child rearers' and the 'careerers', with both casting disapproving glances at the others.

Workplace success and accomplishments are great aspects of life but if we become consumed by these as end goals we can lose our sense of ourselves. Because we are so action oriented we don't take the time to listen to the perspectives of others or even to parts of ourselves. This loss of intimacy with parts of ourselves will be concealed for a time by the prizes of prosperity.

Our working lives offer us a sense of control and progress but it can also lead us towards distraction and avoidance of other relationships. Our telescopic focus on the one goal may mean we do not consider other factors that may result in different outcomes than the one we seek. We then fail to foresee potential obstacles or alternative outcomes.

Tragedy is not an essential companion of success but it is something to be wary of. The point is not to avoid accomplishment but to have a very clear view of what success is for you and to consider what the impact of attaining that success will have on your life.

The terror of forty

A common response to mid-life is resistance and denial. If reaching the age of thirty is unthinkable for the fledgling adult, the prospect of hitting forty strikes terror into the hearts of many people.

Body angst robs many women of creativity as they cram themselves into tight underwear and body control suits and squeeze themselves into dresses.

The big Four-Oh! as one person described it. For most of human history, many of us would never have attained our fortieth birthday. After your fortieth birthday every time you wake up your body must ask, 'Are you still here?'

After forty years of building an identity, serious questions arise about what purpose that identity serves. What is the point of all of this?

There can be a morbid preoccupation with ageing and death. Sorrows and jealousies can afflict people at this time. Losses often cluster. Sorrows may come in the form of death of parents, loss of friends, illnesses, infertility or failure to attain promotions, advancements and opportunities. The pain of grief and loss can etch lines of sadness across your face.

Just as Rembrandt painted shadows to create a sense of light in his artworks, we need to use times of sadness to highlight the joys of life. It is important not to flinch away from sadness and it is just as important to take its lessons and live your life. However, the slumped, sighing ache of loss can become engrained if you are not careful.

> *'One of the symptoms of an approaching nervous breakdown is the belief that one's work is terribly important.'* – Bertrand Russell

Letting go to live more

It is easy to see everyone else's life as problem-free and simple. One piece of advice at this time is to be kind; most of the people you meet are also having a pretty rough time of it.

Allocating your life's energies becomes important at this time. Look at how you are currently allocating yours. If your life's energies were equivalent to thirty-five eggs, how many would you place into a basket called work? How many into a basket called family? How many into a basket called self?

Between 36 and 42 years of age:

- Louisa Alcott, 36, publishes *Little Women* in 1868.
- At 36, Maria Montessori opens her first Casa di Bambini in 1907.
- Sylvia Pankhurst, 36, campaigns for women's suffrage
- John Cleese, 36 develops the comedy series, *Fawlty Towers*.
- Oscar Wilde, 36, writes his first play, 'Lady Windermere's Fan'.
- Georges Bizet writes the opera *Carmen* in 1874.
- Marilyn Munroe dies aged 36 in 1962.
- Mozart dies at 36 in 1791.
- Raphael dies at 36 in 1520.
- Cole Porter, 37, writes 'Let's Do It' later voted the most popular song of the 20th century.
- At 38, Aristotle gets married.
- William I wins the Battle of Hastings, 1066, and becomes King of England at 39.
- Jack Benny reaches 39 and remains 39 for the rest of his life.
- Neil Armstrong becomes the first person to walk on the moon 39 in 1969.
- Marcus Aurelis becomes Roman Emperor at 40 in 161 AD.
- Francis Drake, English sea captain and pirate, 40, rules the seas.
- George Eliot, 40, writes her first novel.
- Virgil, 41, writes the *Aeneid*.
- Lucille Ball gives birth to Desi Arnaz Jnr at 42.

Of course, there is no right or wrong answer. There is no one way to live a life. It is just a matter of asking yourself: is this the way I want it to be? If not, how would I prefer it to be?

In the midst of the rush of life, we can lose sight of ourselves. Willpower and the busyness of life can predominate and we become determined to accomplish the tasks at hand. This might be getting the babies bathed and settled, the investment portfolio reviewed, the work task finished or, recently, all three at once.

The paradox of this stage of life appears to be that at the very time when willpower peaks, we need to learn not to demand the world work in the way we wish. Regardless of how powerful you might feel or how important the projects you have undertaken are, the world was not designed with your personal fulfilment in mind. By loosening your grasp on outcomes, you are freed from innumerable worries. As the Zen teaching koan instructs, 'hold on tight with an open palm'.

This means allowing people to live their lives in their own way, not demanding that they act in certain ways or meet specified standards. The number of dinner parties of this age group that discuss investment opportunities and the right schools to send children to is mind glazing.

By letting go, we find the joy of living. We can continue the work of discovering who we are. By directing some energy in this direction people can open up their own creativity and inner world.

Mapping your life

At this stage, it is useful to be aware of the patterns of your life to date and your predictions about your future. Most people spend more time planning their annual holidays than they spend thinking about the patterns in their lives.

> 'When the past no longer illuminates the future, the spirit walks in darkness.'
> – Alexis de Tocqueville

Having knowledge about the patterns of our lives is empowering because the future belongs to those who plan for it. While no-one's life is so neat that all their plans will be met, at the same time burying your head in the sand and not thinking about it at all makes no sense.

I know that it is tempting, when reading a book, to flick past an activity thinking, 'I don't want to write in the book so I'll come back to that.' Try to give yourself some time to do the following exercise. Grab a big piece of paper, a medium amount of time and a large amount of privacy, and create a map of your life as outlined below.

The vertical axis is your level of happiness and the horizontal is the years of your life divided into seven-year stages.

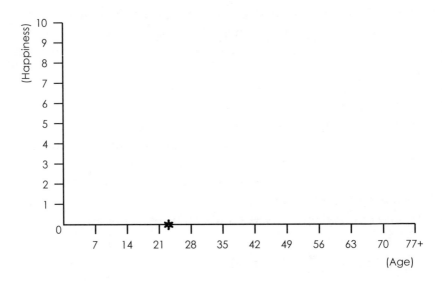

Place an asterisk (*) next to the age your same sex parent was when they had the next child in your family (even if it was a miscarriage or stillborn). If you are a man, this is the age your father was; if you are a woman, the age your mother was. If you are the youngest or an only child, place an asterisk next to the age your same–sex parent was when there was the first major family change after your birth (relocation, job loss, change of marital status, death, illness).

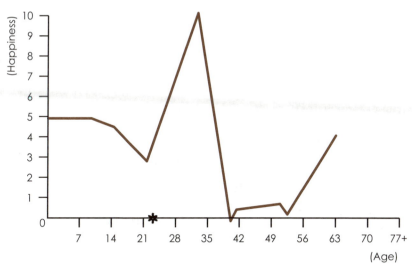

Then map your happiness over your lifetime, with 10 equalling the happiest you have been and 0 equalling the saddest you have been. Everyone should have at least one 10 and at least one 0. Underneath, write the main events that have occurred. Go into your future and map your expected level of happiness for the years ahead.

Have a look over the graphic representation of your life. Do you notice any patterns or recurring effects? Some people find that the age their same-sex parent either had the next child or experienced a family change to be a time of change in their own lives.

You may like to consider:

- What is the future you would like?
- What would this life map look like for your mother?
- What would this life map look like for your father?

If you can, do this map several times, each time deepening your recollections. You may find that memories bubble up – some good, some bad.

You are you because of all of the things that have happened to you. Even if your past includes some terrible happenings, they have still contributed to who you are. You are not your past, however. Giving yourself time to construct the map of your life helps to create a sense of awareness. Having done this process with thousands of people it is clear this exercise helps us to focus on creating a great future.

> Groucho Marx to a woman: 'How old are you?'
> Woman: 'Approaching forty.'
> Groucho Marx: 'From which direction?'

I had, I suppose, reached that moment when well-settled people set out for a second visit to their youth. Mine was a place I had never seen before, having been too involved with children, 'undefendeds', overdrafts and getting on in the law. Gauguin gave up his bourgeois life and set sail for Tahiti. Many men, I imagine, travel the same route, and if their South Sea Island is only the adolescence they never enjoyed, it is subject to the same disadvantages, heat, disease, disillusion, loneliness and the slow disintegration of life in the tropics. I suppose it's possible that Gauguin might have painted his pictures of the South Seas while still living with his Danish wife and during his spare time from the bank. Such considerations never dissuade anyone from attempting the journey, however much they may regret arriving at the destination.

John Mortimer.

36–42 Clinging to the wreckage

Avoid:
- Being sedentary.
- Being sapped of your dreams and energy.

Prepare for:
- Growth and turbulence.
- Success: think about what that really is for you.

Do:
- Know what you want – take time out in a frantic world to think and plan.
- Most people spend their lives reacting to events and changing circumstances. Think about the outcomes you want and write them down somewhere private.
- Practise pathological simple mindedness – once you have an idea of the impact you want to have, focus your energies on it. As most people are scattered, a clear, directed energy often gives you clarity and can help you achieve the outcome you want.
- Hold your own counsel – use fewer words. The world does not need to know your views and thoughts on everything.
- Guard and manage your reputation. Your reputation is your most powerful ally. Your image is within your control. Be conscious of how you want to appear to others.
- Be humble – let your actions speak for you. Be generous. Give credit where credit is due and sometimes where it is not due as well.
- Highlight similarities and conceal differences with other people. Look for ways to have something in common with most people who are important to you.
- Step off the well-trodden path. While still highlighting similarities with others, do things in your own way. Create a distinctive style that attracts attention.
- Be bold.

Read:
- *Too Soon Old, Too Late Smart: Thirty Things You Need to Know Now* by Gordon Livingstone.

Holding the tiger by the tail (Ages 43-49)

Santa Claus has disappeared. Prince Charming turned out to have halitosis. The white horse has a limp. The Easter Bunny has hopped off. Damsels are more distressing than distressed, and the tooth fairy is looking a bit dodgy.

You are in control but only just. The demands of others take precedence over your own issues. You are holding the tiger by the tail.

We live in a time when many people in their forties are simply exhausted. Women are often emotionally depleted from providing for everyone else. Men, in the process of providing for families or striving for success, may also forget to look after themselves. Life at this stage is often over-scheduled and under-nourished by things of the spirit. Timetables, schedules, to-do lists and diaries can rule life.

The maddened frenzied race from appointment to meeting and back again can leave you gasping for breath and yearning for excitement. Just getting out of the door in the morning can be exasperating. Getting back in the door and getting everything organised can be even worse.

> *'Every man over forty is a scoundrel.'*
> *– Bernard Shaw*

Letting your spirit catch up with you

There is an old African story about some explorers who marched into the interior of Africa with several porters carrying their luggage. In three days they had travelled great distances. On the fourth day, however, the porters wouldn't budge. It didn't matter how much the explorers cajoled or offered to pay them, the porters simply would not move. Finally an exasperated explorer asked the porters why they would not move. The answer was, 'We are waiting for our spirits to catch up with us.'

Finding time to pause, to let our spirits catch up with us, initially feels inconceivable to people in this stage of life. Yet the cost of not pausing is great damage to your relationships, not only with those you love but also with yourself. If we lose a relationship with ourselves, our dreams, we become empty and vulnerable to depression.

This is often a turbulent time for people. For men it is peak onset time for heart disease. For women the next seven-year period is heart disease risk time. Interestingly, it is a time when matters of the heart, matter to the heart.

Turbulence can be caused by trials and troubles but it also be caused by growth. Women who manage to re-gather their spirit at this time find themselves surging ahead, often to the bewilderment and threatened response of the men around them. Women often grow through participating in additional education or training, joining

At 43 years of age:

- John F. Kennedy becomes US President.
- Paul Gauguin arrives in the South Seas.
- Dante Alighieri starts work on the *Divine Comedy*.
- Katherine Hepburn stars in *The African Queen*.

At 44

- Stalin takes control of Russia.
- George Washington makes the declaration of independence.
- Margaret Thatcher has her first Cabinet position.

At 45

- Julius Caesar invades Britain.
- Abraham Lincoln starts his career as a politician.
- Virginia Woolf writes *To the Lighthouse*.

At 46

- Benjamin Franklin experiments with a kite in a thunderstorm.
- George Orwell writes *1984*.
- Catherine the Great starts taking younger lovers.

At 47

- Admiral Nelson wins the Battle of Trafalgar.
- Charlie Chaplin stars in *Modern Times*.

At 48

- Harold Wilson becomes British PM.
- Mark Twain writes *The Adventures of Huckleberry Finn*.

At 49

- Oliver Cromwell executes Charles I.
- Tolstoy completes *Anna Karenina* and suffers from depression.
- Leadbelly's first concert.

clubs or groups, and engaging in conversations with other women, which are very different to conversations between men.

The acquisition of objects occurs for many people at this time. Larger television sets, faster computers, bigger houses, flashier phones, all symbolise the success of life. Others turn to obsessive diets and gym training to try to fight off the enemy lines of ageing.

Men who look beyond the acquisition of the symbols of success can deepen their associations with themselves and eventually with others. It is interesting how often men seem unable to do this alone but need to be guided by women. A transformative woman often plays a major role in allowing a man to renew himself in mid-life.

> 'It was only in my forties that I started feeling young.'
> – Henry Miller

The unlived life

On the surface all can look fine, but for many people there is the beginning of a gnawing and a yearning. The unlived life starts to demand attention. It is almost as if there is someone whispering at the back door of your heart: 'Psst, you said you were going to do that and you never have; you wanted to do that and you haven't yet.' Books with titles like *100 Places to Visit Before You Die* leap out at you.

It is particularly in mid-life when passions previously projected onto partners, children and careers wane. Many men and women then miss a grand opportunity to develop a vibrant, mature identity by blaming others for their discontent and do not think to look inwards.

Obviously this confusion creates great pain for the partners, the children and an enormous disruption in people's lives. The failure to differentiate internal anima from external romance and the failure to distinguish being in love from loving someone, has dire consequences for families. But it has tragic outcomes for the individual.

Mid-life crises are all about your anima (feminine playfulness and spirit) surging in an attempt to be expressed. It is as if the anima pounds on the door of your life and if you don't give it room it expresses itself indirectly through symptoms such as depression, bitterness, loss of meaning and/or substance abuse.

For some people a restlessness arises that shakes the foundations of relationships. The initial crack is a wakeup call to take stock of things that are truly of value rather than to throw out things (or people) who appear to hold you back from exploring love and passion and art and beauty.

One of the keys of this stage of life is learning not to blame someone else for the shortcomings of life, but instead to do sufficient inner work on yourself to become the person you need to be in order to live the life you want to live. It is a time to know that, for example, no matter how famous you become, there will always be times when you feel lonely; no matter how much money you have, income alone will not create happiness.

People often speak of having fewer friends at this time. The sifting and sorting of friends resembles the sometimes bloodthirsty process of 'special best friends' around eight or nine years of age.

It is a time to ask yourself clearly and firmly, 'What would success look like?' Define in no uncertain terms your own meaning of success.

Crossing the threshold into a new world

Crossing the threshold of mid-life, there appear to be two extreme pathways that both men and women follow:

1. A collapse of courage and vitality with a scrambling to hold on to the status quo, sometimes even reverting to old ways of being. If on a path of status quo, you tend to surround yourself with people

who hold you back, which results in a long-term path to rigidity.
2. An awakening to potential, acquiring new experiences, skills and interests.

During the later forties, women often gain a new relationship with their own power. The tiredness that accompanies breastfeeding and early child-rearing is usually lessening and many women can reacquaint themselves with friendship groups.

> 'The mark of the immature man is that he wants to die nobly for a cause. The mark of the mature man is that he wants to live humbly for one.'
> – Wilhelm Stekel

The inner-masculine drives of determination and ambition to forge their way in the world benefit women powerfully at this time. It seems that the relationship a woman has had with her father is important in how she will cope at this time. Women who have never shaken off the view of her father as protector or attacker may revisit these issues in relationships with men of their own age.

Women who have dismissed their own mothers, viewing them as passive and ineffectual in the past, may find that they reappraise them at this time.

There is a crossover phenomenon when men and women reach mid-life. They begin to reclaim the powers and prerogatives that have previously belonged to the opposite sex – women can be more assertive, playful and sociable.

Men may enjoy the fruits of their labours at this time. Having worked long and hard, many men are finally in a position to influence others and have some sway. Others become more vulnerable and emotional at this time. For some, their private view of themselves as a cross between an Adonis and Peter Pan begins to wear a bit thin. Broad-mindedness is swapped for a broader waist. Testosterone lowers and hairlines recede. Feelings bubble to the surface.

Men can become a bit sooky at this time of life. A head cold becomes a medical emergency. They may withdraw from friends and become increasingly reliant on women to provide the fun, play and excitement in their lives.

Some become isolated and depressed homebodies, others become terrified of their female partner's growing strength, sexuality and independence. For many men the solution is to work harder, provide more and to fall asleep or drink more to avoid sex.

> *'The true enemy is your failure to love enough.'*
> *– Thaddeus Gola*

People in same-sex relationships are no better off. Two women, if they have not resolved issues with their fathers, can create a hothouse of entanglement that stifles and suffocates them. The clash of unresolved masculinities between two women living together can be harsh and dramatic. Two men who live together may respond by having sex with many partners or fearing that their partner is having wild times without them.

If career setbacks are added to the mix, trouble often looms.

Some people in unsatisfying relationships commence the process of psychological separation during this time. While living together, they create separate lives. For some the primary purpose of taking a promotion, working long hours or starting a course is to get away from their partners. They become increasingly distant and live parallel lives to their partners.

The lesson of Scrooge

One of the salutary lessons for this age is the story of Scrooge in Charles Dickens's *A Christmas Carol*. While hopefully we have not been as pinched and mean and miserly as Scrooge, the story nevertheless provides us with a necessary wake up call.

In *A Christmas Carol*, we find Scrooge is already in a state of living death. It is Christmas Eve and Scrooge is demonstrating his usual mean ways by rejecting his nephew's invitation to dinner, refusing to donate to a charity for the poor and threatening to dock one day's pay from his clerk, Bob Cratchit, for his proposed absence the following day.

Scrooge is then visited by three ghosts: Christmas Past, Christmas Present and Christmas Yet To Come. Christmas Past shows him how he transformed from a pleasant young man into a solitary monster obsessed by money. Christmas Present shows him various happy families enjoying Christmas and Christmas Yet to Come shows him his future – dead, unmourned, unloved and forgotten. He transforms by recognising it is time to construct more positive relationships.

Whether Dickens's story resonates with you or not, this is a great time in life to broaden your relationships and to deepen family connections and friendships. This is the time of life to repair relationships. By this stage of life, almost everyone will have inflicted enough of himself or herself on the world to have created some collateral damage. It is time to clean up the mess as best you can.

A sense of guilt and feelings of hurt can intertwine at this point. Guilt about things we have failed to do or people that we have let down. Hurt about the carelessness of friends and loved ones. This combination of negative emotion can produce inactivity that results in a festering consolidation of these feelings. The solution to the problem is not to avoid these feelings. At this stage of life, you need enough gumption, courage and bravery to tackle problems head-on.

Take action! Remedy what can be remedied and then move on.

Look at the table on the next page and ask yourself the four questions in regards to a troubled relationship you have.

Relationship repair kit

Name of person:

What would I need to improve the relationship?	What should I keep doing?
What should I stop doing?	What should I start doing?

Now ask yourself: what would be the first indication that the relationship is starting to improve?

Slowing down and speeding up

Between forty-two and forty-nine, change is often forced upon you rather than caused by you. As we slow down, time seems to speed up. We have the 'big' birthdays: forty, forty-five, fifty. There is the departure of children, illness or death of parents. People in mid-life go out less and therefore have less social interaction. There can be a feeling that one gives more than one gets. Life may feel pinched.

We become accustomed to developing and progressing as adults, but now, in this time, there may be changes without development. Sometimes there is also a litany of injustices and repetitive rituals of accusation and surrender that endanger relationships. Bitterness, resentment and jealousy can plague people if they wander into the territory of blaming others.

So this stage of life is about overcoming resentment and learning to love. Loving yourself well enough to ignite your creative, passionate, playful side and loving other people well. If you have sacrificed yourself for others you will need to find new ways to declare yourself in your own right.

The realisation of mortality and the loss of belonging come most strongly when someone close to us dies. For some people there is a breakdown of their physical power at this time. Even within a romantic relationship, people can experience a sense of despair and knowledge that mortality lurks just around the corner. This was beautifully expressed by Dorothy Parker's lament:

Razors pain you
Rivers are damp
Acids stain you
And drugs cause cramp
Guns aren't lawful
Nooses give
Gas smells awful
You might as well live.

The trials and tribulations of this stage of life are contributed to by the complexity of the modern family. I was delighted to discover an excellent definition of the modern family by Delia Ephron:

Your basic extended family today includes your ex-husband or -wife, your ex's new mate, your new mate, possibly your new mate's ex, and any new mate that your new mate's ex has acquired. It consists entirely of people who are not related by blood, many of whom can't stand each other.

To expect any one individual to satisfy every aspect of your life is a completely unjust demand. Too many people make a prison of their relationship – and then feel they have to break out of it to be free. The two great tasks of this stage of life are firstly to hold yourself in great esteem while holding on to the good in people; and secondly to realise that the answer to exhaustion is not always rest, it can be wholeheartedness or, in other words, creating a life in which you can wholeheartedly do things you believe in.

Mid-life is also often mid-career, a time where people are prone to burnout. People can slot into several stereotypical roles at work: the frenetic, the world-weary warriors or the under-challenged. There is often a resistance to changes at work during this stage as many people look to work to provide the one constant.

By this stage of life we have coped with enough painful relationships, made enough tense decisions, been fired often enough to have become canny and self-protective – if we pause long enough to think about it. The life we think we are looking for may not be the life we are looking for at all. In this stage of life, people are so time poor they don't reflect on what they really want.

> 'There are old divers and there are bold divers but there are no old, bold divers.'
> – Broome pearling industry saying.

Regeneration occurs in human life just as it does in nature. The withered tree and the dying flower are replenished by the spring.

Men's lives can be so intertwined with work that it may be here that they first feel middle-aged. The younger males are nipping at their heels. By contrast, a woman may look 'good for her age' but feel robbed of her femininity. With menopause there is an increased vulnerability to depression.

Caring for teenage kids and ageing parents may add to the stress of this time. Plans get blasted out of existence by job changes, loss, deaths, family changes and everyone else's needs.

Loving yourself well will help dissolve your ego. You will no longer need to feel superior. You will no longer feel you have to be driven onwards to achieve more and more.

Long service leave without the leave

This is a great time in life to take long service leave without the leave. For a period of six weeks act as if you were on long service leave. Take time out of the wild hurly-burly of life to visit friends, see movies, take walks and make time to catch up with yourself. As Joan Anderson recommends in her wonderful book, *A Weekend to Change Your Life*, it is a time for the Six Rs: retreat, repair, retrieve, regroup, regenerate and return. While you may be too busy to retreat for very long, you may be able to integrate small retreats and mini-breaks into your daily life and enrich your world by acting as if you were on long service leave.

There are literally parts of you that need to die before you do. Taking time to recognise what those parts are takes reflection and consideration.

Between forty-two and forty-nine, life is often frantic. People often don't just lose touch with the people they are in relationships with, they lose touch with themselves. If they don't take some time out to reacquaint themselves with who they are, they mindlessly rush about repeating the same errors faster and faster.

As Carl Jung once said, 'Thoroughly unprepared we take the step into the afternoon of life ... but we cannot live the afternoon of life according to the programme of life's morning – for what was great in the morning will be little at evening, and what in the morning was true will at evening have become a lie.'

> 'Why are you so unhappy?
> Because ninety-nine per cent of what you think,
> And everything you do,
> Is for yourself,
> And there isn't one'.
> – Wu Wei Wu

> The oracle at Delphi inscribed two messages, 'Know thyself,' and, 'Nothing too much'.

Shattering the reciprocity rule

One of the shocks that often occurs at this time of life is the shattering of the belief in reciprocity. This is the idea that good things should happen to people who are good. Scratch the world's back and it will scratch yours is the theory. Many people work hard doing good things and hope that the world will protect their family and loved ones. It's a reasonable trade-off; a fair expectation. The only problem is that it doesn't work.

When dreadful things happen to good people, they can feel shaken, betrayed and embittered. Life has let them down in a personally vengeful way. Their zest for life evaporates and they are left like desiccated zombies trudging monotonously through the routines of life.

As sad as it is to see someone's spirit be dampened, there is an essential lesson that all people have to learn: *We don't get what we deserve, we get what we look for.*

Life disappoints us because it does not work the way we think it should. At this time we need to take charge of what we can control, which is our own perspective.

> 'First there is fear, then there is anger. From anger comes hate and from hate comes suffering' – Yoda, Phantom Menace

People get what they look for in life. You may have noticed this in people you have met. People who look for betrayal in others often feel jealous. People who look for avoidance and lack of consideration in others often end up feeling they need to be in control. People who look for anger in others often end up with fear. People who look for reassurance from others often end up in greater uncertainty. In contrast, look for the best in others and you will often get it.

The second lesson we all need to contend with is: *Give to other people what you would like to receive yourself.* If you would like more playfulness in your life, you need to be playful toward other people. If you would like more love in your life, the best way to have that happen is to be more loving to others. This is a lesson that can take people a lifetime to learn.

> *When I was young and free and my imagination had no limits, I dreamed of changing the world: as I grew older and wiser I discovered the world would not change, so I shortened my sights somewhat and decided to change my country, but it too seemed immovable. As I grew into my twilight years in one last desperate attempt I settled for changing only my family, those closest to me,*
> *But alas they would have none of it!*
> *And now I realise as I lie on my deathbed, if I had only changed myself first, then by example I might have changed my family. From then, by example, I might have changed my friends. From their aspirations and encouragements I would have been able to better my country, and who knows, I might have even changed the world.*
>
> Inscribed on the tomb of an Anglican Bishop at Westminster Abbey.

'People who wait for roast duck to fly in mouth will wait for very long time' – Old Chinese Proverb

The message here, of course, is: change yourself first. This requires freeing ourselves from the shackles of comfort, such as complacency, self pity and inertia, and stopping seeing others as obstacles to our own growth and development.

Viewing the impediments to a better life as only being outside ourself becomes self-limiting. Thinking that others need to change, not us, often results in endless attempts to have others understand you better. It is preferable to direct your energy towards creating the life you want to live. We must recognise that not everything can be changed or improved; some things just require awareness and acceptance.

Why dilemmas are good for us

Life is not simple and many of the quandaries that perplex us are not easily resolved. Life has a way of presenting us with paradoxes. Two or more options may present themselves and there is no clear way to choose between them. This occurs clearly in many relationships when one person wants one thing while the other wants the opposite. The phrase to be 'stuck on the horns of a dilemma' is a common experience for many people.

It is not just in relationships that these paradoxes occur. Often two choices present themselves to people and there is no way of clearly choosing between them. Life can't always be neatly sliced into right and wrong, superior and inferior. Thank goodness it is not so simple.

One of the great steps towards becoming a complete person is shifting from the moral certainties of the twenties where judgement is clear, to a stage of life in which we can encompass ethical dilemmas where answers are unclear. This ability may be viewed as an evasive unwillingness to take action by the 'clear headed' young adult but in fact allows people to move from a situation where options are either 'this or that' to a situation where opposite choices can be viewed as compatible and reconcilable.

Holding two seemingly mutually exclusive options in mind and allowing both to remain in your awareness without making a decision is often a helpful strategy. It is almost as if your mind conducts a conversation between the two options and eventually resolves it; not by opting for one or the other but by transcending both to develop a third choice.

It is precisely this lesson, Christopher Booker, author of *The Seven Basic Plots*, persuasively argues, that many stories are trying to tell us. Transforming yourself often means confronting a series of ordeals or trials. It is not coincidental that in many stories ordeals occur in threes. Jack climbs the beanstalk and enters the giant's castle three times. Genies often give three wishes. Christ spent three days between crucifixion and resurrection. When the Argonauts arrive in Colchis to claim the Golden Fleece, King Aetes tells Jason he must face three trials. Goldilocks has three bears, three bowls of porridge and three beds to sleep in. Gollum poses three riddles for Bilbo to solve in *The Hobbit*. There are Three Little Pigs, Three Billy Goats Guff and so on.

Life is not simply a matter of choosing one thing or another. It is this broader appreciation of the complexities of choices in life that allow people not to simply discard their past but to embrace it and use it to transform their lives.

This ability is what allows people to successfully navigate the next seven-year cycle.

43–49 Holding the tiger by the tail

Do:
- Find missions, causes, jobs and a life you can give yourself wholeheartedly to.
- Develop time and management skills.
- Take mini-breaks and retreats so you can get a glimpse of who you are.
- Look for the best in yourself and in other people.
- Appreciate the richness of your relationships – they are your true wealth.
- Begin to practise the art of minimalism. Although you still have great energy sometimes less really is more.

Avoid:
- Exhaustion and depletion.
- Developing an either/or mindset to life.
- Waiting for other people to change so you can. Go first.

Prepare for:
- Change of priorities.
- Reflecting and sitting back so that you understand changes rather than powering through them.

Read:
- *It's Not About the Money: A Financial Game Plan for Staying Safe, Sane and Calm in Any Economy* by Brent Kessel.
- *First Things First* by Stephen Covey, A. Roger Merrill and R. Merrill.
- *The E-Myth Revisited: Why Most Small Businesses Don't Work and What to Do About It* by Michael E. Gerber.
- *Facing the Fifties: From Denial To Reflection* by Peter O'Connor.

The agony and the ecstasy (Ages 50-56)

Traditionally people became grandparents at this age. What do they do now? I'll tell you one of the things they do is to come to therapy. Carl Jung once observed that more people enter therapy around the age of forty-nine than at any other age. My own clinical experience backs up this observation.

The reason people flock to therapy is that the early fifties is often a life and death battle. The battle is between Thanatos (death and destruction) and Eros (the life force). The way that people resolve or avoid this battle determines the rest of their days.

For people who had rotten childhoods this can be a renaissance time; a time to recapture their lives. If one's childhood was robbed by abuse or neglect, or adolescence was lost through early parenthood or your parent's death there are genuine opportunities here to heal and renew.

By fifty, one has reached the prime age for stable and consistent growth. What was on the horizon in the previous stage of life now steps on to the main stage. You will have to find a new way of being.

There is a test of courage on offer here. The courageous have the impetus to take risks in life; the timid may briefly recapture the playfulness of earlier years before sinking back into the pedestrian mainstream. Fifty is a really good time to ask yourself: 'Who do I want to be when I grow up?'

Many people seem to take on superficial rituals at this time. Many women buy a sports car, get a tattoo or piercings, start wearing purple or add red to their hair. Men often rekindle old passions (e.g. The

---

At 50 years of age:

- George Orwell comments that at 50, everyone has the face he deserves.
- You were old enough to be the head of the curia (200 BC), the original assembly and forerunner of the Senate.
- Degas comments, 'Everyone has talent at 25; the difficulty is to have it at 50.'
- Errol Flynn dies.
- Jacques Tati directs the film *Mon Oncle*.
- Leonardo da Vinci completes many of his greatest paintings. In his 50s he sketches the helicopter, the glider, designs for bridges, windmills, ships' hulls and compasses.
- Henry VIII has his fifth wife Catherine Howard executed.
- Rembrandt becomes bankrupt.

At 51

- Da Vinci paints the *Mona Lisa*.
- Raymond Chandler writes *The Big Sleep*.

Blues Brothers getting the band back together). Men start sniffing around Harley Davidson shops, shaving their heads and becoming 'modern bald' or buying a lot of lycra and going cycling.

This is the time of life people go through their address book and delete names.

Rites of passage

What is going on here is a rite of passage. Rites of passage are not minor blimps on the radar of life. They are opportunities when we can re-consider our direction in life and transform ourselves. For many people this is an unsettling time. As Peter O'Connor noted in his wonderful book *Facing the Fifties*, this is a time of liminality, of uncertaintity and without a clear direction in life.

The rites of passage that occur throughout our lives are particularly powerful between fifty and fifty-six. Arnold Van Gennep wrote about rites of passage in

At 52 years of age:
- Attila the Hun reaches the height of his campaigns against the Roman Empire.
- Brunelleschi designs the Pazzi Chapel in Florence.
- Graham Greene writes *The Quiet American*.

At 53
- Cole Porter writes 'Every Time We Say Goodbye'.

At 54
- Queen Elizabeth I oversees the defeat of the Spanish Armada in 1588.
- David Lean directs the film *Lawrence of Arabia*.
- Abraham Lincoln wins re-election as president.

At 56
- Adolf Hitler suicides at 56.
- Julius Caesar dies.
- J.S. Bach fathers the last of his 20 children.
- Handel writes *The Messiah*.
- William Randolph Hearst starts building his castle at San Simeon, California.

1909, but in reality these reach much further back into human history and culture.

Rites of passage have a sequence of stages:

1. Separation from your normal way of living.
2. Liminality – this is a stage of being betwixt and between, usually confused and all at sea.
3. Return and re-integration.

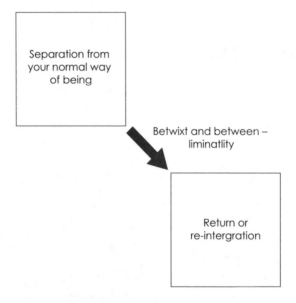

Many of the great works of literature follow this pattern. The first stage, separation from your normal way of living, may be an actual event that alters your life – a trip, a reunion, a shift in life – but most importantly it is really an internal event within your own self. You are in the process of shedding the skin of your previous identity.

The middle phase is liminality. This is a time when people are often seriously confused. They don't know which way to go. They are like the sailor who is lost at sea. Our world has very little tolerance for confusion and unsettled emotion in adulthood. We either send people off for therapy or medicate liminality as depression. Our lack of understanding of this process results in some people blaming it on their partners.

Certainly some relationships have run out of puff by this time of life and separation may be inevitable. Even so, it is awfully easy to blame someone close to you for your own unsettled feelings and to ignore the need to do the inner work needed to create a new you.

> 'The body is at its best between the ages of thirty and thirty five; the mind is best about the age of forty-nine.' – Aristotle

Liminality is sacred space. If used well it has enormous power and opportunity. People who can tolerate a time of ambiguity and uncertainty often discover new interests that fulfil them. If ignored, medicated or trivialised, a great possibility for your future is missed.

The final stage is return or re-integration. This is about making sense of the experience and finding a new you. The entire process of a rite of passage varies in length – for some people it can occur swiftly, for others the process can take years.

Tools for the journey

For people going through a rite of passage at this time, there are three vital pieces of advice:

1. Do not pretend to know who you are, rather, allow who you are to emerge. Guard your soul. Life will be intolerant of your uncertainties. It will want you to fix yourself. Take 'you' time. Preserve your flexibility. This is a time to let ideas simmer. If life at this age is a race between the hare and the tortoise, practise being the tortoise.
2. Old maps don't help you to travel over new territories. The old strategies are not going to work. You are actually going to have to work out a new way to live your life.

3. Contain your blame. You will feel unsettled and confused. At times this will feel unfair and painful. You will blame someone for these feelings. Try not to express this but instead take on the job of overcoming those things in yourself that you feel are not right.

The Western world lacks markers for navigating this phase of life. We live in a popular culture that is ignorant and disrespectful of ritual and sacred passage. This lack of knowledge can cause great pain for people and their partners going through this experience.

> 'He who hesitates is a damned fool.'
> – Mae West

It is helpful to recognise that others have passed this way before. There are many examples of separation, liminality and return in our culture. Homer's *The Odyssey* is one such example, in which Odysseus leaves Ithaca and endures many perils before eventually returning to his home. Significantly on his return he is so changed that initially not even his family recognise him.

Tolkien's *Lord of the Rings* also follows this pattern. It details the journey of Frodo and Samwise Gangee from the Shire to toss the ring into the fires at Mordor before they return homeward. Other examples of journey and return include Lewis Carroll's *Alice's Adventures in Wonderland*, H.G. Wells's *The Time Machine* and Jules Verne's *Journey to the Centre of the Earth*. Even the *Star Wars* series of films follows this process. These and other stories tell us something fundamental about human experience; it is crucial to go and lose yourself in order to forge a new self.

We often think of this rite of passage as a conquest in which the hero (generally male), heads out from home and slays a few dragons before returning older and wiser. However, the challenges do not have to occur as a physical test; they can be a broadening of life. Examples of this type of experience include Dervla Murphy's travels, The Bandit Queen's rebellion, Robyn Davidson's journey across Australia on camels, the Buddha's prolonged meditation under the Bodhi tree and Tenzin Palmo, the Buddhist nun, who spent twelve years in a cave.

The new identity formation that needs to occur in this phase of life is not inevitable. Some people get stuck and become adolescents again. Up until this point for most people life has been a matter of opposites – either rich or poor, happy or sad, allies or enemies, male or female, in my group or out of my group, local or foreigner. This over-simplistic view of the world always causes a roller-coaster effect – you feel either up or down. For once you decide on one end of the continuum you necessarily bring about its opposite. For example, as soon as you decide you are happy there will be other times when you will be sad. Overcoming either/or thinking and encompassing multiple perspectives allows us to transform ourselves.

Getting yourself back together

The divided self has been discussed in many texts. From 700 BC onwards, the Upanishads contended that the divided nature of human consciousness meant we are imprisoned in Maya, the state of illusion, but within us is atman, our true self. In Chinese philosophy, the yin and yang considers the balance of two opposing forces: male and female, light and dark, strong and weak, solid and fluid, creation and completion, idea and realisation. These two forces are ultimately integrated and transcended by Tao or 'the way'.

To bring forth a full mature identity requires us to meld the two forces of our inner male and female aspects into one expanding sense of who we are. It is time to go an archaeological dig to unearth the parts of you that have been submerged along the way. To do this well we need to understand that old ways of doing things will no longer be sufficient.

Accomplishing this archaeological sifting for the discarded parts of yourself requires you to remove yourself from the busyness of life. There has been a long history of retreat

> 'What a strange machine man is. You fill him with bread, wine, fishes and radishes and out of him comes sighs, laughter and dreams'
> – Nikos Kazantakis

and renewal in many lives, including Mohammed, Jesus, Buddha, Dante, St Paul and Gregory the Great.

All of the great writers in this area – Joan Andersen, William Bridges, Frederic Hudson, Maureen Murdock and Joseph Campbell – all agree that taking some time for yourself is an essential part of this process.

Eight steps to reinventing yourself

This is not a leisurely holiday designed to rejuvenate or replenish yourself – though that may be useful at some point too. You are not broken or in need of refuelling. This is a time for reinvention of yourself.

There are eight steps to this process.

1. Realise that the changes that are needed are internal. You can save yourself and those you love a lot of anguish and pain if you realise the way out is in. Don't discard external relationships until you find out who you are. Give yourself some time to do this.
2. Still yourself – the temptation is to remain busy. We rebel against the idea of retreating for a time, partly because we are so addicted to the busyness of life. It is tempting to fill the emptiness with increased busyness, telling ourselves there are people who rely on us, who need us to keep scurrying on the treadmill of life. Listening to these messages comits us to more and more exquisite forms of the same torture. At some level we are aware that we are experiencing an ending and endings are symbolic of death. It can be scary to sit back and let things happen when we have been so used to controlling the pace and outcomes of events.
3. Go away for a weekend or a few days by yourself. Try to go somewhere beautiful where it is unlikely you will bump into people you know. Try to maximise the opportunities you have for reflection. Switch off the phone, don't take distractions such as DVDs or TVs. This is not the time to catch up on that favourite book.

4. Don't try to achieve anything during this time. Don't look for an outcome. There are no deadlines. Let your mind off the leash. Let it wander about sniffing at new possibilities and softly focusing on issues. Avoid massive physical challenges during this time. Hiking and climbing mountains is well and good but there is a risk that you will simply replace one form of busyness with another. Take care of yourself during this time. That midnight swim in the ocean could be your last.
5. Keep an eye out for coincidences and omens. Joan Andersen writes of going down to the beach to sit and watch the ebbing tide before she realised that ebbing was exactly what she needed to do.
6. Keep a journal of your thoughts and observations, even those that make no sense. Having done this myself several times and having worked with many people going through the process, there is a common experience; people describe feeling almost completely uncertain about the outcomes of this time while also feel utterly themselves.
7. When you come back don't feel obliged to talk about it. The people around you may feel anxious and ask you to account for your time. If you try to explain it you may find yourself saying things like, 'Well, I'm not really sure what I got out of it,' or 'Nothing really happened.' These explanations may diminish the experience for you. A retreat is a work in progress, not an end in itself.

Prepare people in advance for your time away by saying something like, 'I'm going

> 'Passion is powerful. Nothing was ever achieved without it and nothing can take its place. No matter what you face in life, if your passion is great enough, you will find the strength to succeed. Without passion life has no meaning. So put your heart, mind and soul into even your smallest acts. This is the essence of passion. This is the secret to life.' – Anon

away for a few days to sort a few things out for myself. We are fine and I am fine and I need to do this. I won't be contactable but I will be back.'

8. After your return, try to find some time each day for silent reflection. Use gardens, libraries, parks and churches. Again try not to strive for an outcome. The result, if there is one, is your own self-awareness. Slowly, gently, by giving yourself space in your life to listen, you begin to unearth the voice that is truly yours. At first it will be barely a whisper, no louder than the beating of your heart. But over time it will grow in strength. It is that voice that, if given time to develop, will tell you what is truly important for you.

While this process of rite of passage is well observed in literature, it did not trouble many of our ancestors for the simple reason that many of them did not live to be this age. What people do around fifty years of age impacts greatly on their long-term wellbeing. If we look at what predicts healthy ageing at age eighty, several factors at age fifty emerge:

- Stable relationships
- Avoiding cigarettes
- Modest use of alcohol
- Regular exercise
- High education
- Maintaining normal weight

To this I would add the ability to make lemonade from lemons. When tough things happen, learn how to make the best out of them. Best wishes to those of you who try it!

Oh no! I'm a teenager again

There is an interesting mirroring between this time of life and adolescence. Issues, confusion and passions rise to the surface in a way that is similar to our experiences in our teenage years.

People who were not able to experience adolescence fully because of family demands, cultural constraints or other circumstances may find this to be a renaissance time in their lives. This mirroring is not accidental – it is because both groups are embarking on the business of identity formation. Both age groups are working through the four main ways of developing a new identity: moratorium, achievement, confusion or foreclosure.

It is a time to regain passions. By this age half of American women are divorced, widowed or single. The amount of dislocation, and in some instances sheer misery and loneliness, is mind-boggling.

> 'If it wasn't for me, I would do brilliantly.'
> – Chamfort

If you are tearing up a marriage and trying again it will be at fifty. You might have actually emotionally torn it up years before but it's at fifty that people do something about it. If you can get a new hold on life at this age, you'll have grace and nobility.

While some relationships do run out of puff, it is too easy to feel unsettled at this age and to blame the restlessness on a wife, husband or partner. By pointing a finger and proclaiming 'it's over' we can adroitly miss a great opportunity in life to turn inwards and reinvent ourselves. This can lead to what I call the Curse of Don Quixote. Cervantes's *Don Quixote* is a story of the foolishness of a man who projects onto the outside world a battle which should have been fought inside him.

The emergence of a new quest, such as a new job or new relationship, can energise and vitalise at this time of life. However, the most important quest is inside rather than outside yourself. Loving yourself well now sows rich crops to be harvested later.

How to become your own assassin

People can become their own assassins at this time. Some actively wish away their lives: 'Only two days to the end of the work week; Only one month till I can take holidays' is a lament heard in many workplaces.

> *'The graveyards are full of indispensable men.'* – Charles de Gaulle

I often feel like adding, 'Only several years to death,' whenever I hear someone wishing away their lives in this manner.

Other people create toxic and eventually fatal relationships. If a woman is prone to heart problems it often begins here. The risk is a loss of vitality.

Pressures include invisibility as sexual desirability and attractiveness change; the loss of children as they leave home lessening the energy in many homes; the possible or real loss of meaningful work. Others feel stuck in jobs that are mindless and repetitive and feel they must hold out for their superannuation or pension.

When asked how they are, many people in this age range answer, 'busy' or 'not bad'. If asked what they have been doing they answer, 'not much'. Grimly holding off life at this time for the prospect of better times to come is to practise being dead prematurely. Successfully negotiating this age is to recognise the realities of mortality and to then practise active exuberance.

It is almost as if people of this age range should carry two pebbles in their pocket. On one pebble should be inscribed the message: 'The world was created for you to be free in!' But on the other pebble should be inscribed the message: 'You are dust!' It is holding both realisations in your mind and then getting on with living life well that is the key.

There are four main rules or realisations that allow people to live a great life at this time:

Rule 1: Anything is possible.
Rule 2: Nothing is easy.
Rule 3: When everything is going well, remember rule 2.
Rule 4: When everything is going badly, remember rule 1.

The art of deep nourishing relationships of all types is the wellspring of joy at this time. Take time to build friendships and connections that nourish and delight you.

During this phase of life you will meet your devils. You can try to run away from them but they will chase you and hunt you down. The big question is: Will you decide to let them move in with you?

50–56 The agony and the ecstasy

Do:
- Practise self-reflection.
- Change and deepen your sense of who you are.
- Realise that you will need to invent new ways of doing things. Previous ways will no longer work.
- Become a great lover – of partners, family, friends.
- Develop your sense of humour – make lemonade from lemons.

Avoid:
- Blaming others.
- Discarding people – partners, friends.
- If you experience depression get it treated and use the treatment to move more powerfully into life.

Prepare for:
- Expansion through creativity and love.
- Holding life more lightly and reaching beyond your grasp.

Read:
- *Twenty Good Summers* by Martin Hawes.
- *Lifelaunch: A Passionate Guide to the Rest of Your Life* by Frederic Hudson and Pamela McLean.
- *Crossing the Unknown Sea* by David Whyte.

Regeneration or degeneration? (Ages 57-63)

You have strived hard, had a few close calls, a few wild times, been a good friend, wrecked a few good relationships, stood on a few toes, brought a twinkle to an eye or two. Death has robbed you of a few loved people.

Many people no longer know what you are talking about when you speak about the songs, stories and movies you loved as a youth. The 'celebrities' featured in glossy magazines are often a mystery to you. The unlived life that started whispering at the back door of your heart in your forties now starts to yelp, 'Time is short, youth has passed its bloom, last drinks, ladies and gentleman!' In the shake of a moment you seem to have gone from forty to almost sixty. One day you're

> 'Their teenish tricks, at fifty-six
> All wise folk should forego'
> – Anon, c.1800

blazing a path towards maturity, the next you realise you are there.

You may even wonder to yourself, 'How did I get to be a bit over the hill when I can't remember reaching the top?' Are you better to hold on grimly to those last few vestiges of youth fighting a rearguard action or slip into the comfortable padded slippers of seniority?

The renaissance of the soul

It is during this phase of life that a critical decision is often made: to regenerate or degenerate. Thaddeus Golas in his wise book *The Lazy Man's Guide to Enlightenment* advises the basic function of each being is expanding and contracting. Expansion is awareness, connectedness, love and understanding. Contraction is felt as fear, pain, ignorance and hatred.

To be healthy and resilient, life needs to be expanded at this time. Open-mindedness is the key to expansion and enlightenment. If you do not expand your life at this point, you run the risk of selling yourself short, playing it safe and deadening your spirit.

Insecurity at this age is unsettling. The desire to play it safe and acquire money for retirement satisfies the ego that wants you to deny that times are changing. This dive for the eiderdown of comfort is well described by Lawrence Durrell when he wrote of the tree of Idleness in Bellapias in Northern Cyprus. People of a certain age were careful not to drink coffee under it lest they were 'forever consumed with idleness'.

Life begins to change but it doesn't have to mean a narrowing of interests, relationships or pursuits. Part of you should resolutely refuse to grow old; it should be like a coach giving you a pep talk, saying, 'C'mon, you're at the peak of your powers, there's time for many victories yet. You're too young for bowls, bingo or gardening.'

As Martin Hawes comments, it is a time to plan to have at least twenty more great summers. It is also a time to build strength as whatever you do, the body eventually will present its bill. This is the time to maintain vitality and strength.

It is also a time when the senses can dull. Eyesight can dim. Hearing may become patchy. Tastes are less distinctive and aromas less entrancing. We know from many people who have lost a sense that this is an aspect we can train ourselves to become more sensitive in. Increase the acuity of your senses. A woman I know has a boyfriend who had a dreadful accident, and as a result of his injuries he lost his sight, his sense of smell and taste. Despite this she took him out to the finest restaurants. I was incredulous until she explained, 'You wouldn't believe the pleasure he gains from the textures of the food.'

Rather like a gourmet who dines on the finest foods, you might like to engage in a revelry of the senses. Seek out the most bewitching and entrancing aromas. Walk through freshly cut grass, sniff out the summer rain, absorb the haystack smell of baby's hair or the salt of the sea or the smell of asphalt after rain. Hang around bakeries in the early morning.

Become an observer of beauty and delight in the world. Let visual beauty touch you. Find art that enchants you, sculpture that makes your fingers yearn to caress, and dance to music that makes you want to stomp and leap.

Know the wonderful light-fingered stroke of love, feel the strength of massage, the firm greeting of a good handshake, the textures of materials. Hug and be hugged.

Open your ears to the music that makes your heart twang, your feet tap and your hips sway. Discover poetry that creates harmonic resonances within you and the sound of laughter.

Taste new foods. Eat slowly and notice the interplay of tastes on your tongue.

By simply observing, noticing and becoming more aware you open yourself to expansion. Exploring the world beyond your usual

> 'Life is a handful of short stories pretending to be a novel.' – Anonymous

routines and placing yourself outside your usual comfort zones increases the zestfulness of life.

This is also a time to regard employment warily and to find work close to your spirit. The drudgery of bad work can kill you. Now, not everyone can resign and go start a bed and breakfast or a new business, nor should they. It is about finding something that is important to you to do and then doing it. This requires from us contribution and commitment.

To open ourselves to new pursuits we need to downsize our egos. This means lessening the amount of our identity that is invested in work and individual accomplishments. In the language of corporate downsizing, whole departments of ourselves can either be let go or taken out the back and dealt with.

This does not mean retreat. Instead it is an advance into deeper relationships and more meaningful endeavours. As Howard Thurman, the American theologian put it, 'Don't ask what the world needs. Ask what makes you come alive, and go do it. Because what the world needs is people who have come alive.'

To find what makes you come alive, you have to lessen the impact of those things that deaden you. You need to free up new real estate space in your life. It is time for a shake-up, time to get even more interesting.

Freeing yourself up is like doing an internal stocktake: 'What do I need to get rid of? What do I need to add? What do I need to give away?' If we decide to keep too much of our former lives we stay burdened by outmoded routines and risk destining ourselves to more tiredness and emotional depletion. If we rid ourselves of too much we risk being isolated, lonely and unfulfilled.

Where we place our attention is crucial at this time. Focusing on those things that tire us, such as requirements, obligations and drudgeries, is a short-cut to death. Be mindful that it can be easier to complain about the necessities of continuing a dull life than to create and re-invent ourselves.

Mythologist Joseph Campbell points out that there is an important choice between placing your attentions on a declining body that may not be what it once was or on the consciousness and aliveness that the body contains. As he puts it, 'Am I the bulb that carries the light or am I the light of which the bulb is a vehicle?'

Less achieving, more being

This shift in focus from achievement to just being is not easy and our set ways don't go quietly. Men may find their ego squawks and shrieks and won't want to leave. Equating happiness only with achievement can sentence people to a lifetime of work without meaning if they are not careful. Men who have been taught to tame or hide their feelings may be overwhelmed by moodiness or grumpiness for a time. It is hard to look the prospect of career irrelevancy fair and square in the eye.

Women may find they can finally look after their individual needs after years of nurturing everyone else. However, some may be so addicted to providing for and organising others they can't stop. If they can shift from 'doing for' to 'being with' as expressions of love and caring, feelings of freedom and fearlessness may emerge. However this can be undermined if they are drawn into the world of parenting, rather than grandparenting, their own children's children.

To become the hero or heroine of your own life you need to summon the positive qualities necessary to wrench and wrestle with life-giving feminine values from the shadows of your life. As Robert Johnson puts it, to be the hero or heroine of your own life requires that you have both the harp and the sword.

Men and women in this stage of life also need to access the masculine energies of power and strength, mastery and independence, and to gain a sense of order, propriety, discipline, justice, rational wisdom and compassion. These give a backbone and vigour to human life. There is great value in holding life firmly in the cross hairs of your vision. Being clear and being fearless are ways of summoning your powers.

The strength and power of the masculine has the potential to become hard and inflexible if not counterbalanced by the inner feminine. It is this balance that links power with connection to others, a world outside the ego.

Develop outward masculinity and inner femininity. Think of Gregory Peck in *To Kill a Mockingbird* and Katherine Hepburn in *The African Queen*. Be caring and sensitive but when it is time for actions, act decisively.

> Billy Connolly's advice to men turning 60 is: 'Never pass up an opportunity to pee; never waste an erection, even if you're on your own; and never trust a fart.'

There is often a rough patch of internal squabble before creativity can be found. Yoggi Berra's advice that 'when you see a fork in the road, take it!' seems good guidance here.

Taking the fork in the road requires you to realise there is not just one you. Your 'self', as you might call it, is really a gathering of multiple possibilities. There is the mean you, the nice you, the humble you, the kind you, the obnoxious you, the dreamer you and so on. If you have taken time to rise in a career or raise or provide for a family, you will have presented the world with a fairly consistent you. Other parts of your self dropped out of view along the way. You may have even begun to think that was all there was to you.

It is easy to dismiss those parts of you by ending sentences with the phrases 'But I'm grown up now,' or, 'But I'm too old now'. For example, 'I used to love going on surfing trips, but I'm grown up now,' or, 'I always wanted to visit Jerusalem, but I'm too old now.'

This is not a time to go easy on yourself. It is a time to recapture those parts of your self that have passion and delight and creativity.

In Australia, groups of people in this age range and older travel around the country in vans and trucks. Collectively they are known as the 'grey nomads'. The grey nomads have a saying: Adventure before dementia!

Creativity can turn an older person into a young person and is an important tool for dealing with ageing. Creativity has to do with unburdening, with opening the doors and windows of your life and letting new air, new projects, adventures and activities in. As Joseph Campbell put it, you need to spend a part of each day when you don't know who you are. It is a time to get busy living.

Creativity is not a singular activity – that leads to rigidity. There is a vast difference between opening up your life to creativity and what can be called hardening of the categories. You will have met people who have begun to suffer from hardening of the categories. They make comments like, 'It's Tuesday night, we play bingo.'

> 'Art is your personal contribution to the ongoing conversation of life.'
> – Ronnie Burkett

Regular activities are not the problem. The risk is using scheduling, in a life that has more than likely spent so many years being scheduled by other people's wants, to deny yourself new experiences.

Humans love patterns. We use them to survive every day. We do much the same things in much the same ways over and over again. Patterns make life expedient in that we don't have to invent new ways of doing things every time. The trouble is that some patterns that are useful in earlier phases of life are no longer applicable in later life. As one female participant in one of my workshops commented, 'I was so successful at organising everything that any offer of help was superfluous. Then one day I realised I had actually organised other people out of my life. I presented such a "perfect" face to the world there was no room for anyone else.'

One man commented, 'I became the magician who thought he had to have an endless supply of rabbits in his hat. I saw my family

At 57 years of age:

- Geronimo surrenders to the white man.
- Immanuel Kant writes *The Critique of Pure Reason*.
- Bernini starts constructing the piazza and colonnade at the front of St Peters.
- Auguste Rodin produces his sculpture of Balzac.
- The Earl of Cardigan leads the Charge of the Light Brigade.

At 58

- John Milton publishes *Paradise Lost*.
- David Lean films *Dr Zhivago*.
- Isaac Asimov publishes his 200th book and Georges Simeon starts writing his 180th book.

At 59

- John Brown liberates slaves at Harper's Ferry, Virginia in 1859.

At 60

- Tolstoy celebrates the birth of his thirteenth and last child.
- Eleanor Roosevelt becomes a delegate to the United Nations in 1945.

At 61

- Harry S. Truman orders the atomic bombing of Hiroshima and Nagasaki in 1945.

At 62

- Louis Pasteur creates the first injection against rabies.
- Linus Pauling wins the Nobel peace prize.
- David Niven's autobiography *The Moon is a Balloon* becomes a best seller and he commences a second career as a writer.
- Walt Disney produces *Mary Poppins*.

At 63

- Wagner sees the first-ever performance of his *Ring* cycle.

as an insatiably needy group that needed me to provide them with money. The only problem was that as long as I saw them that way, I was going to work myself into an early grave and resent them.'

It takes a fixedness of intention to break open some of those patterns, and your life may feel uncomfortable at first.

Throughout history, humanity has needed different forms of creativity to express imagination and a sense of the divine. In the Middle Ages, creativity was mainly expressed through architecture and gothic cathedrals; in the 15th and 16th century Renaissance, it was through painting and sculpture. In the early 17th century the focus moved to literature acted out on stage – the plays of Shakespeare and the poetry of John Donne and John Milton and *Paradise Lost*. By the 18th century it was music, Bach and Handel, Haydn and Mozart, and then Beethoven and Schubert. In the early 21st century it is film and computers.

The same is true for people: one form of creative expression may not be enough. One part of your self may no longer be enough. You may well need to seek a variety of ways of expressing your spirit and creativity. You may need to accept that you are more complex as a person than you have previously been prepared to show the world.

Re-acquainting ourselves with beauty

In order to see beauty it is necessary to allow ourselves to be touched by other people and to be able to identify with them.

You don't need to wander off on a pilgrimage, become an ascetic or join a movement. You can just pay attention to whatever magic, aliveness and curiosity you've got.

The broadening of your self may come as a bit of a shock to those around you. Early on it may be unwise to discuss this too openly. The changes you start to make will either unsettle them or they will deny them entirely.

Alternatively they may be truly shocked by the new ventures you are embarking on. For those of us with children, realise your children have an enormous amount invested in you being consistent. Children, especially in their twenties, can be disparaging and outraged by their parent's perceived irresponsibility.

Friends may be similarly perplexed. If a friendship falls on hard times, try to buy some time for it by saying, 'I'm sorry, I'm just working things out for myself at the moment.'

Luke Rheinhart's book, *The Dice Man*, in which he shatters the confines of consistency by choosing life options with the roll of a dice, is worth reading at this time.

Broadening yourself doesn't mean that you go off on some ego-driven, self-indulgent, hedonistic experience at the expense of others. Quips such as 'spending the kids' inheritance' are amusing but miss the point. The purpose here is not to threaten or disrupt important relationships; it is to increase the amount of relating that you do with others.

People who have lived much of their lives, caring and providing for others, may need to broaden the range of people they are friends with. It may be necessary to 'run with a larger pack' despite the disapproving glances of your family.

> 'What a wonderful life I've had! I only wish I'd realized it sooner.' – Colette, novelist

Establishing new regimes and habits between fifty-seven and sixty can prolong life. It seems our society has a greater tolerance for women doing this than men. Many women form a community together. Men often struggle to find others to share adventures with after they have sacrificed friendship for career success.

This time does not involve giving up your job. Instead see your life's work as larger than your job. Create what author David Connolly calls 'a career path wide enough for your life'.

The ancient Greeks made a distinction between 'animal' work, which is necessary to stay alive but leaves behind no lasting contribution, and 'human' work which casts your true being into the arena of life and through which you make a courageous difference. This is the time of life to undertake work that is worthy of you and to place that work very close to your spirit. Salvador Dali, Carl Jung, Mahatma Gandhi all did their best work at this stage of life.

Setting your sights high and enjoying the journey is part of living a great life at this time. It has been magnificently captured in the poem 'Ithaka' by C.P. Cavafy:

As you set out for Ithaka
Hope the voyage is a long one
Full of adventure, full of discovery.
Laistrygonians and Cyclops,
Angry Poseidon – don't be afraid of them:
You'll never find things like that on your way
As long as you keep your thoughts raised high,
As long as rare excitement
Stirs your spirit and your body

Laistrygonians and Cyclops,
Wild Poseidon – you won't encounter them
Unless you bring them along inside your soul
Unless your soul sets them up in front of you

Hope the voyage is a long one
Nay there be many a summer morning when with what
pleasure, what joy
You come into harbours for the first time;
May you stop at Phoenician trading stations
To buy fine things,
Mother of pearl and coral, amber and ebony
Sensual perfume of every kind –
As many sensual perfumes as you can

And may you visit many Egyptian cities
To gather stores of knowledge from their scholars.

Keep Ithaka always in your mind
Arriving there is what you are destined for
But, do not hurry the journey at all.
Better if it lasts for years, so you are old by the time you reach
the island
Wealthy with all you have gained on the way
Not expecting Ithaka to make you rich

Ithaka gave you a marvellous journey
Without her you would not have set out
She has nothing left to give you now
And if you find her poor, Ithaka won't have fooled you
Wise as you will have become, so full of experience,
You will have understood by then what these Ithakas mean.

57–63 Regeneration or degeneration

Do:
- Take new adventures.
- Try creative and bold undertakings.
- Take time to re-cap and renew.
- Keep your brain and body active. Learn new skills, make new friends, travel if you can.

Avoid:
- Slipping into set patterns and routines.
- Bitterness.
- Hardening of the categories – doing the same things in the same ways.

Prepare for:
- Expansion through creativity.

Read:
- *Ageing Well: Surprising Guideposts to a Happier Life From the Landmark Harvard Study of Adult Development* by George Vailliant.
- *Transformations: Understanding the Three Levels of Masculinity* by Robert Johnson.

Intimacy or invisibility? (Ages 64-70)

Resignation or retirement doesn't mean retreat from life. It is a great mystery why some people use this time as a jumping-off point for the rest of their lives while others shrink into invisibility.

Being older doesn't mean giving up on life, yet some people try for invisibility at this stage. They adopt a 'below the radar' lifestyle as if keeping quiet will protect them from loss and grief. It almost seems they think that if they stay indoors, keep quiet and lie doggo that death will somehow forget about them.

It is amazing that we can be surrounded by death and yet pretend that it will never happen to us.

Many of the infirmities that traditionally accompanied this age have largely disappeared through medical and health advances. Certainly there is the odd dodgy back and dicky knee, but most of us can expect to get through this stage of life battered around the edges a bit perhaps, but intact.

The concept that people of this age should think about leaving work full-time is a relatively new one. The idea that retirement should happen at sixty-five began with German Chancellor Otto von Bismarck in 1884, when very few people lived as long as we do now.

The dread that some people feel at the prospect of not being involved in a regular workplace is more often than not, a sense of grief. Grief can lower your immunological functioning and make you sick. This is why we see some people who are vibrant and full of beans fall apart and die quickly once they leave work.

> 'Two weeks is the ideal length of time to retire.'
> – Alex Comfort.

Retirement is not for everyone. This is why retirement, if done at all, needs to be a gradual process.

Men are especially vulnerable if they have not prepared for this time. Many of them equate stopping work with decline and they turn retirement into a death sentence. Others replace the battles of the workplace with fierce competition on the golf course or tennis court. Feelings of depression and discontentment invade their lives. If they have not opened themselves up to creativity in the previous seven-year phase, they often feel obsolete.

> 'One starts to get young at the age of sixty and then it is too late.' – Pablo Picasso

Ernest Hemingway apparently suicided when he could no longer live up to his own bar-trawling, hunting, macho image.

Failing to reinvent themselves, many men and increasing numbers of women continue the fast peddling of age denial. Norman Mailer told a wonderful story about age denial. Mailer and his wife were at a function. Mailer looked at his reflection in a nearby mirror and mentally noted that he looked pretty good. At the luncheon Mailer and his wife met Mohammed Ali. Ali was courteous and chatted pleasantly with Mailer. Ali flattered Mailer by saying 'You look great!'

Feeling terrific, Mailer excused himself to go to the toilet. After he departed Ali turned to Mrs Mailer and asked, 'What are you doing still hanging around with that old man?'

> *'If you want to escape the heat jump into the fire.'*
> *– Buddhist proverb*

The shock of realisation that you are the age you are and no-one is going to be fooled by how many races you win or trophies you acquire can seem very rapid. As one man told me, 'I moved from being a wise man to an old codger in a matter of weeks!'

The art of having a twinkle in your eye

> *'Human beings, who are almost unique in having the ability to learn from the experience of others, are also remarkable for their apparent disinclination to do so.'*
> *– Douglas Adams*

This can be a time of great intimacy and of deep friendship. It is a time to begin to cultivate discernment about what is truly important as well as keeping a rakish twinkle in the eye. This is the time to pull the plug out of the power source and to connect into world-changing projects. Rather than pretending to be ageless, this is the time to become an old dog and to learn new tricks.

Perhaps in your family there has been a role model you can use. Someone who has gleefully embraced life at this time. They are often the distant relatives others tut tut about. You know, the grand aunt that sweeps in with flowing scarves and massive earrings, gives everyone a dollar and chortles her way out. Or the roguish uncle who takes up greyhound racing and dubious company and always has a bottle of beer for breakfast.

At 63 years of age
- Tolkien publishes *The Fellowship of the Ring*.
- Anaïs Nin publishes her diaries.
- Alfred Hitchcock makes *The Birds*.

At 65
- Casanova starts writing his memoirs.
- Voltaire writes *Candide*.
- Giacomo Cassanova starts writing his memoirs.

At 66
- Kenneth Clark creates his *Civilisation* TV series in 1966.

At 67
- Freud completes *The Ego and the Id*.
- B.F. Skinner writes *Beyond Freedom and Dignity*.
- Tolstoy has his first bicycle lesson.

At 68
- Gregory Bateson writes *Steps to an Ecology of Mind*.
- Ginger Rogers does three weeks of shows with the Rockettes at City Music Hall.

At 69
- Ronald Reagan is elected US President.

At 70
- Golda Meir is PM of Israel.
- Socrates is forced to poison himself for leading astray the youth of Athens.
- Tolstoy rides 20 miles and makes love to his wife to celebrate his birthday.
- Marlene Dietrich tours Australia.

It is time to be a 'character'. Shaking off the shackles of other people's expectations can free you to do this. Looking at the colourful aspects of your personality and deciding to play up to them can be a good idea.

Even if you are not so extroverted, exuberance is still worth cultivating. If there is a time in life to become quirky and interesting, this is it. Life is a performance. It is time to take your place on the stage.

Aim for gracefulness but not necessarily decency. Create lifelines for change: take action, have an adventure, face your fear, seize the moment, tolerate isolation and, as Joan Andersen in *A Weekend to Change You Life* says, reach beyond your grasp.

Associating with younger people at this time is good for the soul. It is wonderful to know that dignity does not exclude fun. Stand out from the crowd by refusing to complain and by creating a mind set of 'Why not?'

One apocryphal story that relates to this age is the Long Jumping Jeweller of Lavender Bay. A mild jeweller living an industrious life catches the ferry across the Sydney Harbour to work every day. One morning he is late and has to jump to catch the ferry. People notice; some applaud. Each day the jeweller times his arrival at the ferry pier a fraction later so he has to jump slightly further. People are urging him on, placing bets on his jumps, he becomes a celebrity. His formerly dull life has been given purpose.

Sadly the inevitable happens and one day he times his arrival so late that the jump is impossible and he falls into the harbour. The next morning, quietly dressed, he arrives at the ferry in time to board it in the usual manner.

To take a leap is admirable but to land on your feet is something all together different.

Don't be subdued or shamed back into a tame existence. The disapproval of people you know, and children if you have them, can be a force for conservativism. It may work well for them to have you

> 'If I had any decency I'd be dead. Most of my friends are' – Dorothy Parker, 1963

exactly the way you've always been but it won't work well for you. You thrive best when you reignite your wilder side. The people who do this stage of life best recapture the child-like spirit that has often been obscured in the years of working and providing.

We know from early childhood that without love, humans do not develop. It is at this time that once again we need to broaden our capacity to love and be intimate. Developing varied, deep friendships with people of various ages is a gift at this time.

Men generally have larger social networks than women but less intimacy. The concept of having deep conversation and connection can seem foreign to men who have been used to the hit-and-run nature of business relationships.

When death comes

When death comes
like the hungry bear in autumn;
when death comes and takes all the bright coins from his purse

to buy me, and snaps the purse shut;
when death comes
like the measles-pox;

when death comes
like an iceberg between the shoulder blades,

I want to step through the door full of curiosity, wondering:
what is it going to be like, that cottage of darkness?

And therefore I look upon everything
as a brotherhood and a sisterhood,
and I look upon time as no more than an idea,
and I consider eternity as another possibility,

*and I think of each life as a flower, as common
as a field daisy, and as singular,*

*and each name a comfortable music in the mouth,
tending as all music does, toward silence,*

*and each body a lion of courage, and something
precious to the earth.*

*When it's over, I want to say: all my life
I was a bride married to amazement.
I was the bridegroom, taking the world into my arms.*

*When it's over, I don't want to wonder
if I have made of my life something particular, and real.
I don't want to find myself sighing and frightened,
or full of argument.*

I don't want to end up simply having visited this world.

Mary Oliver

Men need to learn to treat people as if they are complete and perfect as they are. This includes themselves and it certainly includes their children. Many men address the issue of fathering as if they were running an improvement program for their children. If they persist with this strategy, people will avoid them. People are not problems to be solved or situations to fix.

Women are protected by social networks such as close friendship groups. To broaden their social networks women have to move beyond the 'who's in and who's out' games that can ocurr. It didn't work well in the primary school playground and it certainly doesn't work well at this time.

For some newly retired men the only close friend they have is their wife or female partner. His clinginess can drive her witless (or away). Men who have been enterprising or successful in the business world, often have to invent an entirely new way of relating to people. Used to ordering subordinates, advising children, or instructing anyone within earshot, these men have to grapple with equality in relationships.

In homosexual relationships with the common veneration of youthfulness, this can be a time of turmoil. The fear of loss, anxieties and the trouble of attaining intimacy can mount up. It is not surprising that for many people gardening and bowls seem appealing and a whole more rewarding to boot.

> 'Can't go under it
> Can't go round it
> Got to go through it!' –
> popular children's song

Touch, intimacy and sex are important. Before Viagra, many men had given up the ghost sexually. Erectile difficulties are not part and parcel of ageing but even so, the raging stud of yesteryear may need to learn new methods, becoming more focused on touch, enjoyment and mutual satisfaction. Sex has to be less reliant on erections and penetration and more on being a great lover. Couples re-igniting a sexual relationship that has dimmed through years of work, stress and family need to take the time to develop sexual techniques that do not resemble torrid, adolescent fumblings.

There is a great love and intimacy to be had in deep companionship, whether it be friendship, family relationship or as lovers.

This is a time when the meaning of life should change. To not grow now, is to sentence yourself to a premature death penalty. Don't wait for an illness, a crisis or the death of someone close to you to learn this lesson.

64–70 Intimacy or invisibility?

Do:
- Maintain vitality and muscle strength.
- Join clubs, get involved. Volunteer.
- Harvest the fruits of your labours.

Avoid:
- Feeling too old to be involved.
- Feelings of dispensability.
- Delegating major decisions.

Prepare for:
- Health limitations.
- Independent decision-making about what happens to you.

Read
- *Zorba the Greek* by Nikos Kazantzakis.
- *The Five Stages of the Soul: Charting the Spiritual Passages That Shape our Lives* by H.R. Moody, and D. Carroll.
- *From Age-ing to Sage-ing: A Profound New Vision of Growing Older* by Z. Schachter-Shalomi, and R.S. Miller.

IRONICALLY, THIS WAS ONE OF THE HAPPIEST TIMES IN NORMAN'S LIFE

Dignity
(Ages 71-77)

Most people don't fear being old when they finally get there. They do fear being bored, lonely or being treated as invisible, silly or confused. Loneliness can stem from the lack of close intimate relationships or social networks.

The sense of indignity that can affront people at this age is life robbing. If you are surrounded by people who act as if you are mentally deficient or unable to complete rudimentary tasks it can cause feelings of deep hurt, rage and embarrassment. Extreme embarrassment can kill you years before your time.

There is a lot of bunkum written about this time of life. Despite the prevailing myth that these years are accompanied by fragility and senility, only 5 per cent of people over sixty-five are in nursing homes and less than 10 per cent will ever be. Only 5 per cent of people over sixty-five suffer from dementia.

Psychiatrist Gordon Livingstone wisely says that old age is not for sissies. It's not, but it's also not a time to turn into a dodo. Author and physician Oliver Wendall Holmes, at the age of eighty-four, upon seeing a beautiful woman said, 'Oh to be seventy again!' People are just as smart, switched on and shrewd as ever but the world seems to be intent on labelling them as incapable and old. Ageing does not have to mean growing old.

> 'Do not go gentle into the dark of the night, Rage, rage against the dying of the light.'
> – Dylan Thomas

This is the time of life to insist on being in the world; being part of your community and spending time with people that you love. It is easy to feel that you should really pack yourself off somewhere – to a home, to a gated community (or penitentary for the aged) or to a highly desirable but almost inevitably lonely location.

> 'About this issue of ageing, I want to make a terribly important point. People decide to get old. I've seen them do it. It's as if they've said, "Right, that's it, now I'm going to get old." Then they become old. Why they do this, I don't know. Maybe they like to be dependent. But I do think it's terribly important that people not make that inner decision. Because then they sit around and they're old. It's easy not to do it, in fact. It's not about staying young but about not getting old.' – Doris Lessing

People may want to make arrangements and plans for you. Tell them decidedly to go and get stuffed. There is a dignity in controlling your own destiny.

Others want to be helpful. Let them help but don't let them control what happens to you.

It is a time when the body does not work as it once did. Twinges turn into aches, aches turn into pain, power turns to frailty. Sleep can prove elusive. You may be up roaming in the middle of night and then unable to keep your eyes open after lunch. Names can fail to arrive on your lips. Clarity of purpose can become wayward.

This phase of life is unknown territory. Most of your ancestors did not achieve this age. For most of history people couldn't dream of living into their seventies.

Across history the average life span has varied dramatically. In classical Greece and Rome it was twenty-eight years, in medieval Britain it was thirty-three years, by the end of the 19th century in Western Europe it was thirty-seven. Historically speaking, you are doing very well.

There has been a 50 per cent increase in life expectancy since 1900, especially for women. Despite this, many people use this additional time waiting and ailing and complaining. It is an important time of life to question the contemporary view of ageing, and ask how are you going to use this additional lifetime. Will you embrace life or just spend more time being old?

I was delighted to discover a 1933 issue of *Time* magazine that contained an interview with Li-Chang Yuen, a man who purportedly lived to the age of 256. For those of you interested in attaining this fine age, I include Li-Chang Yuen's four-step formula for living for your consideration:

1. Keep a quiet heart.
2. Walk sprightly like a pigeon.
3. Sit like a tortoise.
4. Sleep like a dog.

Two views of ageing

The traditional view of ageing is that there is a peak in life after which there is a, hopefully, graceful decline. This decline can commence at quite a young age. I had a young man in my therapy room who lamented, 'Well what can I expect, I'm twenty-five now!'

The other view of ageing is that you function fairly well until a few days before you fall off the perch.

Lived well, this can be an expansive time. People of this age group have the financial resources – and are less driven by external demands – to be able to pursue their own interests. Men become less focused on competitive achievement and dominance. Shifting away from the power race can be a wrench for some but a glorious opportunity to spread the wings for others.

Television shows have turned being crotchety and grumpy into comedy. Shows like *Steptoe and Son, Mother and Son, Grumpy Old Men* and *Grumpy Old Women* display the wily wisdom of the senior years.

This is a time to know that life is shortening and to be clear about priorities. I am very fond of the lessons learned along life's rocky road, developed by Sheldon Kopp in his *Escatological Laundry List*:

1. *This is it!*
2. *There are no hidden meanings.*
3. *You can't get there from here, and besides there's no place else to go.*
4. *We are all already dying, and we will be dead for a long time.*
5. *Nothing lasts.*
6. *There is no way of getting all you want.*
7. *You can't have anything unless you let go of it.*
8. *You only get to keep what you give away.*
9. *There is no particular reason why you lost out on some things.*
10. *The world is not necessarily just. Being good often does not pay off and there is no compensation for misfortune.*
11. *You have a responsibility to do your best nonetheless.*
12. *It is a random universe to which we bring meaning.*
13. *You don't really control anything.*

14. You can't make anyone love you.
15. No-one is any stronger or any weaker than anyone else.
16. Everyone is, in his own way, vulnerable.
17. There are no great men.
18. If you have a hero, look again: you have diminished yourself in some way.
19. Everyone lies, cheats, pretends (yes, you too, and most certainly I myself).
20. All evil is potential vitality in need of transformation.
21. All of you is worth something, if you will only own it.
22. Progress is an illusion.
23. Evil can be displaced but never eradicated, as all solutions breed new problems.
24. Yet it is necessary to keep on struggling toward solution.
25. Childhood is a nightmare.
26. But it is so very hard to be an on-your-own, take-care-of-yourself-cause-there-is-no-one-else-to-do-it-for-you grown-up.
27. Each of us is ultimately alone.
28. The most important things, each man must do for himself.
29. Love is not enough, but it sure helps.
30. We have only ourselves, and one another. That may not be much, but that's all there is.
31. How strange, that so often, it all seems worth it.
32. We must live within the ambiguity of partial freedom, partial power, and partial knowledge
33. All important decisions must be made on the basis of insufficient data.
34. Yet we are responsible for everything we do.
35. No excuses will be accepted.
36. You can run, but you can't hide.
37. It is most important to run out of scapegoats.

38. *We must learn the power of living with our helplessness.*
39. *The only victory lies in surrender to oneself.*
40. *All of the significant battles are waged within the self.*
41. *You are free to do whatever you like. You need only to face the consequences.*
42. *What do you know ... for sure ... anyway?*
43. *Learn to forgive yourself, again and again and again and again.*

The seventies are a good time to make friends – especially with yourself.

A touch of recklessness is not a bad thing at this time. It is much worse to feel that you should stay indoors, preserve yourself and gloomily count the increasing numbers of tablets that seem to accumulate in your cupboard.

It is around this time that many people become fascinated with their ancestry and begin constructing family trees and photo albums. It is almost as if by gathering their heritage they are making sense of their place in history.

It is important not to watch too many news shows at this age. Media always takes a proctological view of life and therefore highlights the dramatic and the unsafe. Too much television news is designed to scare the gee willikers out of people. The media play on the insecurities and can convince people at this stage of life that it is not safe to go beyond the front door.

The world may seem deplorably harsh and foolish to you. While there have been massive technological advances, in many ways the human lives you witness can seem emotionally impoverished. It might seem that wherever in the world we are ruled by numbers we lose our connection to our inner selves. The corporate ethic of 'if you can get away with it, it is fine' can dismay you.

At 71 years of age:

- Bette Davis receives an Emmy Award.
- Coco Chanel re-emerges as a leader in the fashion world.
- Deng Xiaoping assumes leadership of China.

At 72

- Charles Darwin publishes his last book.
- Ambrose Bierce goes on an expedition to Mexico and is never seen again.

At 73

- Sigmund Freud writes *Civilisation and its Discontents*.

At 74

- S.J. Perelman, with two companions, drives from Paris to Peking in an old MG.

At 75

- General de Gaulle continues as President of France.
- Morarji Desai, Indian politician, begins a new health habit – drinking a glass of his own urine every morning. By 81 he is Prime Minister of India.

At 76

- Winston Churchill becomes Prime Minister of Britain for the second time.

At 77

- Thomas Hardy publishes a book of 159 poems.
- Ronald Reagan continues as US President.
- Barbara Cartland writes her 254th romantic novel.
- Mae West stars in *Myra Breckinridge*.

Even so, it is time to focus on your personal legacy. Become a wise elder by the way you live your life. There is no point trying to provide instructional lessons. You will feel that you are in old age and full of wisdom no-one listens to!

This is the time to gather whatever gifts you have and give them to the world. It could be the gift of happiness or greeting. It could be knowledge or perspectives. Most of all it will be the way you live this part of your life.

Through providing service to others we enlarge our worlds. It is awfully easy to be swept aside by anxieties and grief at this time. Some friends will die. Decisions can feel hard to make.

Throughout life we are healthiest when our world is expanding. We need to be panoramic, not microscopic. To do this we need to deal with regrets and move on. For all of us there will be things we regret having done, things we regret never having done, as well as things we are happy we have done.

Psychoanalyst Victor Frankl once commented that suffering is like gas. It can take up all the available space in your life. Once we have dealt with regret it is time to turn our heads firmly to the present and the future.

The irretrievable sin is not living in the moment. If you can manage this, it will amaze you that you feel so young at this age.

The delicate beauty of life in each moment is something to be savoured.

> 'When you are in your middle seventies you have passed your peak as a cat-catcher. There was a time – say between 1904 and 1910 – when it would have been child's play for me to outstrip the fleetest cat, but now the joints have stiffened a trifle and I am less quick off the mark.' – P.G. Wodehouse

70–77 Dignity

Do:
- Deepen friendships and companionships.
- Create rituals of connection and pleasure.
- Develop awareness and wonderment.
- Utilise your resources.
- Think about your personal legacy – how can you act in a way that shows the world how to live?
- Be young, be spirited. The world will want you to be old.
- Hug other people well and consider regular massages. Often people in this age group lose their physical connections with others.

Avoid:
- Aloneness.

Prepare for:
- A true connection with the great themes of humanity, the rhythms of nature and the river of ancestry that courses through your bloodstream.

Read
- *Beauty: The Invisible Embrace* by John O'Donohue.
- *Conversation: How Talk Can Change Our Lives* by Theodore Zeldin.

EDGAR WAS EMBARRASSED
ABOUT HAVING WINGS...
HE NEVER TOLD A SOUL
HE NEVER LEARNT TO FLY
IT WAS HIS TERRIBLE SECRET

Contentment and bitterness (Ages 78 and beyond)

I have reigned more than fifty years in victory and peace. During this time I have been beloved by my people, dreaded by my enemies, and respected by my allies. Riches and honours, power and pleasure, have all been at my beck and call, nor has any earthly pleasure been missing to complete my sense of perfect bliss. In this situation I have diligently numbered the days of pure and genuine happiness that have fallen to my lot. They number fourteen.

– Abd-ar-Raham III

In 2000 when the torch was being relayed around Australia before the Sydney Olympics, it arrived in the town of Bendigo and into the hands of the oldest relay runner, Jack Lockett. Jack was 109 years old at the time and completed his part of the relay watched by his four children, the youngest of whom was John, a sprightly spring chicken aged only eighty-five. After his run Jack was asked about his life and he said, 'Well, in my life I've had my worries but I decided not to worry about them.'

I wonder who you would prefer to be more like? Abd-ar-Raham or Jack Lockett. My money is on Jack.

For much of history, ageing has been viewed as synonymous with the acquisition of wisdom. In recent decades, especially in the Western world, older age has been seen as intertwined with inexorable decline; a terminal period of irrelevancy.

Obviously not all older people are wise, nor are all young people naïve. Even so, the failure of the world to draw upon the knowledge, awareness and considered opinions of its most experienced citizens makes no sense. In a world that appears fragmented and sensationalised, to not actively seek out the ideas of people who are able to view matters holistically as well as historically seems sheer madness.

The idea of a decline in cognitive functioning, creativity and contribution in the senior years of life has been over-played. As one woman in the age range said to me, 'You almost feel that unless you have diabetes, osteoporosis, incontinence, absent mindedness and are perpetually inflicting stories of your ailments on to someone else, there is something wrong with you!'

Rather than a necessary decline in physical functioning there is a mental shift in emphasis and direction. Meaning changes dramatically. There is a movement from hierarchy to collaboration, from status and achievement to connection, from aspiration to appreciation.

John Wayne was once greeted by a film hand one day as he came out of his caravan on a film lot, 'Lovely day, Mr Wayne!' the young man exclaimed.

'Son', drawled John Wayne, 'When you reach my age, any day you wake up is a lovely day.'

The shift in emphasis that occurs at this time of life enables ideas to go off in completely new directions. The works of people in their later years is one example. Many great artists have had a late stage of creation which is complex and unified. Often, because it is different from their carlier works, it is initially devalued before later being reappraised as among the artist's finest works.

> Samuel Street dies at 102 disrupting preparations for his sixth marriage. (1774)
>
> Mrs. Watkins dies at 110 having eaten only potatoes since the age of 80. (Wales, 1970)

After 78 years of age:

- Konrad Adenauer, post-war chancellor of Germany, is in office until 87.
- Ayatolla Khomeini replaces the overthrown Shah of Iran in 1979 at 78.
- Matisse creates designs for the Chapel of the Rosary, Venice.
- Goya completes the Bulls of Bordeaux.
- Verdi writes Falstaff.
- Andres Segovia fathers his last child.
- David Lloyd George marries his secretary at 80.
- M.F.K. Fisher writes till her death at age 81.
- Barbara McClintock is awarded the Nobel Prize for her ground-breaking work on cellular biology in her eighties.
- Pablo Casals marries one of his pupils, Maria Montanez.
- Henry Moore has a large exhibition of his sculptures.
- Charlie Chaplin is awarded an Oscar at 83.
- Lee Kwan Yew continues to play a powerful role in Singapore.
- Michelangelo works up to six days before his death at 89. His last twenty years are his most productive producing a design for a chapel in Rome at 84, a design for the Porta Pia at 85 and at 86 a design for Santa Maria degli Angeli.
- Albert Schweitzer works with the lepers in his hospital at age 90.
- Oliver Wendall Homes was on the Supreme Court at 90.

For example, Beethoven's last string quartets use the timbres of the various instruments to create a unified fusion of music. It echoes a world view in which similarities are more important than differences.

The great late works of dancer and choreographer Martha Graham, and the artists Rembrandt, Titian, Michelangelo, Rodin, Goethe Monet and Cezanne, all express a unity of thought and emotion.

The talent of the abovementioned geniuses is rare but there is evidence suggesting that, overall, it is older people who have advantages in emotional intelligence, practical reasoning, the integration of feeling and thought, as well as a greater tolerance for ambiguity.

The transformation in people at this time is best paralleled by the sonata in music. The sonata form usually presents a masculine first part with a steady rhythm followed by a more essentially feminine second subject. The two combine and intertwine through the development section to return transformed and integrated.

In the same way, people who gather both aspects of their inner selves seem to thrive best. The polarised separation of femininity and masculinity are least conducive to wellbeing at this time.

Women who have dieted excessively to maintain the 'right' shape are often struck down by physical weakness, such as osteoporosis. If they have placed all their energies into being attractive and alluring, the 'invisibility' of the senior years can be a shock. Men who have clung to physical power and prowess of their youth and middle age are often afflicted by isolation and depression.

> 'In the depth of winter, I finally learned that within myself there lay an invincible summer.'
> – Albert Camus

Intergrating both aspects of yourself allows you to encounter your remaining years fully aware and with the intention of being alive for every moment. It allows you to connect more richly and more deeply with an appreciation of life in the present.

Also, it seems the prospect of being old which held such fear for so long, loses its sway. For many years people deny their age, avoid birthdays and fight vehemently the signs of sagging and wrinkles. Once you finally arrive at this stage, life can be quite calm. Those battles are no longer worth fighting. In fact, a sense of sprightly playfulness often emerges.

Voltaire was on his deathbed at the age of eighty-three and was asked by a priest if he would like to renounce the devil. His answer was, 'I don't think it's time to be making enemies.'

I was delighted to discover the following epitaph on a gravestone in St David's Park, Hobart:

> *Stranger take heed as you pass by;*
> *As you are now so once was I;*
> *As I am now so you will be:*
> *Prepare yourself to follow me.*

And I was ever more delighted to see that some wit had written underneath:

> *I might but I am not content*
> *Until I know which way you went.*

A life that has been well lived has an immense force behind it. For people with such lives there is a buoyancy about their existence. It doesn't mean that they are spared from suffering, loss and grief but it does mean they have a context for the last phase of life.

> *'Old age is not for sissies.'*
> *– Gordon Livingstone*

This is the time of life to live like you are dying, to connect with the great forces of life. We all have the blood of ancestors coursing through our veins. We are all subject to the great rhythm of human life – its ebbs and flows. We are all part of the seasonal variations of nature. We are part of the life force. This is the time to connect richly and deeply

> 'On my last birthday I was ninety-three years old. That is not young, of course. In fact, it is older than ninety. But age is a relative matter. If you continue to work and to absorb the beauty in the world about you, you find that age does not necessarily mean getting old.' – Pablo Casals

with life and with others, but it is a time to expect some bitterness – don't be consumed by it.

The view that you have of dying is important, especially now. No-one really believes in their own death. Most of us say to ourselves, 'I know that death is inevitable I just thought in my case they might have made an exception.'

No matter how advanced human civilisation has become, the one thing man has no remedy for is death Some people seem to fade away as if death is something to be waited for. Others try to squeeze as much joy and pleasure out of whatever time remains.

Imagine a great death. What would that be like? Would you be surrounded by loving friends and family who would be saddened by your passing but exhilarated by the vivacity of your life, your love and your contribution? Or would you perhaps prefer, as you sigh your final sigh, for the collected gathering to collectively think, 'Well, thank goodness that's over. The old girl or boy has finally fallen off the perch. No more moaning, whingeing and complaining!'

> 'If I die, survive me with such a force You put the pallor and coldness to shame' – Pablo Naruda (from Love Sonnets)

The vision that Shakespeare paints of the end of life being no teeth, no eyes, no taste and no everything is overly bleak. The idea that old age is necessarily a time of deterioration needs to be challenged. The popularisation of this way of viewing these years plays on people's fears of being a burden to their family

Having a sense of home is essential at this time. Home is a place where you control what happens to you personally. Nursing homes treat old age as an illness, fostering dependency, powerlessness and loss of freedom. Even if you have the energy to protest, you still end up complaining without being heard. Frustration or a resigned sense of compliance are not the ways to thrive at this time.

The power of playfulness and hope is beautifully illustrated by the work of William Thomas who became the Director of the Chase Memorial Nursing Home in 1993. From all accounts the Chase Memorial Nursing Home was a fairly dour place before William's arrival. It was a place where people waited to die. William brought dogs, cats, birds and rabbits into the nursing home. He filled the rooms with plants and turned the lawns into vegetable gardens. He invited children from local schools to come into the home and encouraged play. The results were dramatic. Infection and medication rates were able to be reduced by 50 per cent. The death rate dropped by 25 per cent.

> When Sleeping Beauty woke up she was one hundred and sixteen years old.

I once heard a story about an elderly woman got into a taxi. After the driver had assisted her with her bags she thanked him profusely and said, 'I'm ninety-six, young man.' The woman then looked into her purse and said, 'Oh dear, I've forgotten my cab charge.'

The driver responded by saying, 'It's understandable you might forget a few things when you are ninety-six.'

She turned haughtily toward him, arched an eyebrow and enquired, 'Who told you I was ninety-six?'

There is a lot of living that happens at this time if you can stop treating death as an ogre and develop a positive resolve to make the most of each moment. Death is not an enemy. One of the overwhelming experiences that occurs in working with people who are dying is that death is not traumatic. The causes of death can be painful but the process of death is almost always calm and smooth.

Our world conducts a conspiracy of silence around death. The poet Walter Savage Landor wrote magnificently about this:

> *Death stands above me, whispering low*
> *I know not what into my ear:*
> *Of his strange language all I know*
> *Is, there is not a word of fear.*

The fear of death can rob you of your life. We can be so intent on preserving ourselves that we fail to take the risks that bring a spark to life. This is, of course, aided by media that highlights the dangers in the world.

One of the reasons so much publicity is given to famines, crashes, murder, natural disasters, violence and all the other negative information that fills our 'news' services, is that it increases our sense of survivorship. The good news for us, about bad news for other people, is that it didn't happen to us. We evaded death once again. Perhaps, after all, death will never happen to us.

Life is growth. When you stop growing you die. As the old saying has it, 'It's better to die on your feet than to live on your knees'.

The playwright Arthur Miller talked about this in his memoir *Timebends*:

> 'She drank good ale, strong punch and wine And lived to the age of ninety-nine' – Epitaph to Mrs. Freeland in Edwelton churchyard, Nottinghamshire, 1741

> *'I still feel – kind of temporary about myself,' Willy Lomas says to his brother Ben. I smiled when I wrote the line in the spring of 1948, when it had not occurred to me that it summed up my own condition then and throughout my life. The here and now was always melting before the head of a dream coming toward me or its tail going away. I would be twenty before I learned how to be fifteen, thirty before I knew what it meant to be twenty and now at seventy-two I have to stop myself thinking like a man of fifty who has plenty of time ahead.*

Gathering together the threads of your life, sifting the trivial from the essential and seeing a connection between yourself and the ongoing stream of human and natural existence is the key to freedom. People who gain this key gain the gift of being themselves. Aspiration and envy wash away, leaving a sense of being precisely who you are.

> *Do not stand at my grave and weep;*
> *I am not there, I do not sleep*
> *I am a thousand winds that blow*
> *I am the diamond glints on snow*
> *I am the sunlight on reapered grain*
> *I am the gentle autumn rain.*
>
> *When you awaken in the morning's hush*
> *I am the swift uplifting rush*
> *Of quiet birds in circled flight*
> *I am the soft stars that shine at night.*
> *Do not stand at my grave and cry*
> *I am not here*
> *I did not die.*
>
> Mary Elizabeth Frye

78 and beyond – contentment and bitterness

Do:
- Acknowledge death but live life.
- Love others well.
- Be a model of love and closeness.
- Let your good memories warm you and lift your spirit.

- Connect yourself with current events, new ideas and the excitement of future development. Even if your body is ageing, your outlook can be young.
- Playfulness and humour.
- Connect yourself with the great eternal forces and rhythms of life and nature

Avoid:
- Regrets, recriminations and bitterness that can take away the time you have.
- Isolation and rumination.

Prepare for:
- Making the most of every moment.

Read
- *Move Into Life: The Nine Essentials for Lifelong Vitality* by Anat Baniel.
- *When Things Fall Apart: Heart Advice for Difficult Times* by Pema Chodron.

If I had my life to live over

It's such a little thing to weep,
So short a thing to sigh;
And yet by trades the size of these
We men and women die!

Emily Dickinson (1830–86)

Early in the winter of 1832, a twenty-year-old man was about to die. Challenged to a duel the next morning he worked through his last night. Writing at breakneck speed, he paused agitatedly to note in the columns of his treatise, 'I have not time. I have not time.' By morning he had written as much as he could and early on 30 May 1832, went out to duel with pistols at twenty-five paces.

Evariste Galois, mathematical genius, was shot in the intestines. He comforted his brother with the words, 'Don't cry, I need all my courage to die at twenty.' He died the day after the duel and was buried in an unmarked, common grave. The paper that he wrote that night created a mathematical theory that is still used today.

On 21 February 1944, the Hungarian patriot and French resistance fighter Imre Glasz was sentenced to death with fourteen others by Nazi firing squad. In the hours before his execution, Glasz wrote:

> *My little wife Ila and Borsi:*
>
> *These are the last hours of my life. We go before the firing squad at three o'clock in the afternoon. One page won't suffice to write all I'd like. My little Ila, I kiss you and love you infinitely. I hope you'll get better and can yet be healthy. Be as optimistic as I am. I have nothing for which to reproach myself; I have lived like a man and want to die like one. Life has no great value without freedom, and those who don't fight for their life don't deserve it. As for me, I wish for a much better life ... Forgive me for not being a man crying at the edge of his life, but courageous and ready to die. My little Ila, Borsi, little André and Odette, all those who are dear to me. Let all the goodness that I have in me be with you in your life. I kiss you for the last time. A thousand kisses.*

Both these men knew their time was limited. We often live our lives as if our time were endless.

Our journey began with an invitation made by the great physicist Isaac Newton to stand on the shoulders of giants and to look a little down the pathways of life ahead. Perhaps it is also useful to lean on the giants' shoulders and look back and consider what is truly important in life.

If we have any chance at all of distilling the essence of what life has to offer we need to return, as the poet, T.S. Eliot put it, 'to a condition of complete simplicity costing not more than everything.' When we peel back the inconsequential, the distracting and the trivial, what we are left with is the valuable in life.

In the wild rush of achievement and desire and accomplishment, most of us lose sight of our core purpose and calling. We get tangled up in the hurly-burly and excitement of the everyday world and forget to nourish or notice the things that give long-term satisfaction.

The most important parts of life are not for sale or purchase. They cannot be grasped. They are not measurable. They are not even visible. They are, however, essential ingredients for a full and rewarding life.

Pause for a moment and consider the following questions:

- If I were to die tomorrow what would I say to those I love?
- What is in my heart?
- Who would I most want to communicate with?
- What would I want to tell them?
- How would I like to be remembered?
- How will I live on in the memories of others?

The most essential parts of life, of course, are debatable. In workshops and therapy sessions I have discussed this issue with thousands of people and I try below to talk about the main themes. If you would like to contribute to this ongoing conversation, please enter the discussion forum at my website www.andrewfuller.com.au.

Appreciation and gratitude

How can we be surrounded with such abundant pleasures and beauties and yet fail to see them? How can it be that we are given such gifts by those who love us but we forget or discard them soon after they are received? Are we destined to be the victims of our own greedy minds

– the insatiable driven parts of ourselves that are never content and always want more?

There is an old Sufi story of the Mulla Nasruddin, an honourable prankster, who sees a miserable man walking along the road. 'Alas,' cries the man, 'I have lost everything! Poor me! All I have left in life is one solitary bag!'

The best things in life

- Falling in love.
- Listening to rain spattering on the roof while lying in bed.
- Being in an outdoor spa in a rainstorm.
- A warm breeze though your hair.
- Frost on a winter's morning.
- Laughing so hard your sides hurt.
- Watching your sports team win.
- Listening to music.
- Smelling bread baking.
- Thunder over distant hills.
- A hot shower.
- A special glance.
- Having your hair washed by someone else.
- Taking a drive on a pretty road.
- Hearing your favourite song on the radio.
- Hot towels out of the dryer.
- Chocolate milkshakes.
- Receiving a long-distance phone call.
- Making new friends or spending time with old ones.
- Spending time with close friends!
- Discovering that love is more powerful than time.
- Riding the best roller coasters over and over.
- Hugging the people you love.
- Watching the expression on someone's face as they open a much-desired present from you.

The Mulla decides to act quickly and runs past the man, grabbing hold of his only bag, taking it from him.

The poor wretch is overcome with sadness. 'Poor me,' he wails, 'my last, solitary bag has been stolen. I am truly cursed.'

The Mulla sees that the road ahead bends so he takes a shortcut and places the bag in the middle of the road for the man to find.

On finding the bag intact in the middle of the road, the man becomes overjoyed. 'I have my belongings again. I have not been forsaken,' he exclaims.

The Mulla observes, 'See what it takes for a person to be happy?'

Most of us are lucky without realising it. Most of us are far wealthier, in the true sense of that word, than we ever accept. Bringing that good fortune to full awareness and using it to create a way of viewing our lives allows us to be humble and grateful.

The best things in life

- Staying in love.
- Jonquils.
- Magpies chortling.
- Asphalt after rain on a hot afternoon.
- The smell of the desert.
- Mozart's Adagios.
- Fresh linen.
- Hearing an acknowledgement.
- Discovering a shortcut.
- Reading a great book.
- Singing your favourite song at top volume.
- The smell of a home-cooked meal.
- Sunlight through dappled leaves.
- The symphony of a forest in a light breeze.
- The Milky Way.
- A massage.
- Travelling to new places.
- The smile of a friend.
- A hug that lasts and is really meant.
- Music that lifts your heart and pumps your blood.
- The wag of a dog's tail.
- Beautiful wine.
- A raging wood fireplace on a cold night.
- A really great story.
- Discovering a new idea.
- Photo albums.
- Painting and drawing.
- The smell of babies' heads.

Appreciation is an art that can be developed. It is a fundamental and basic outlook on life. Considering yourself to be lucky for what you have is one of the fastest pathways to happiness.

We need to try to emulate the deep compassion and appreciation expressed by a sadly unknown prisoner at Ravensbruck Concentration Camp during World War II.

> 'When I grow up, I want to be a little boy.'
> – Joseph Heller

> Oh lord, remember not only the men and women of good will, but also those of ill will, But do not remember all the suffering they have inflicted on us; remember the fruits we have bought, thanks to this suffering – our comradeship, our loyalty, our humility, our courage, our generosity, the greatness of heart which has grown out of all this, and when they come to judgement let all the fruits which we have borne be their forgiveness.

Appreciation and gratitude are linked to happiness. There are three reasons why you should be happy.

The first is that you were born. What an unlikely event that was. All of your ancestors had to survive to maturity, meet the right person and reproduce so that eventually you could be born. From the turn of the 13th century until today, we each have, mathematically speaking, approximately two-and-a-half-million direct ancestors. They had to avoid early death by plague, war, famine or accident in order to produce you. If you go back ten generations (250 years) the chance of you being born at all is *at most* 1 divided by 6×10^{100}, or 1 in 6000000 00000000000000000000000000000000000000000000000000000 0000000000000000000000000000000000.

The second reason you should be happy is that you are alive right now. Of the 106 billion people who are estimated to have ever lived on this planet, only 5.8 per cent of them are alive right now.

The third reason you should be happy, as Bill Bryson quite rightly points out, is that you live in a time of when the song 'Tie a Yellow ribbon around the old oak tree' will never be number one again!

> *'If I had my life to live over again, I would have a different father, a different wife, and a different religion.'* – John F. Kennedy, US President

Health

Your body is yours to live in and you should develop it so that it will serve you well. Build as much vitality, muscle power and exuberance as you can. During the industrious phases of life, especially from thirty-six to fifty-six, it is important not to disregard your own wellbeing and to continue building your energy.

The simplest way is to recall this is to do your MEDSS:

Meditation – a daily activity where you can let your mind free of the rush of ideas and find who you are behind the thoughts. Just return your awareness to your breath for a time each day.

Exercise – make time each day to work up a sweat and build strength. Exercise may be the single greatest thing you can do to improve your happiness. Studies indicate that even light exercise, if done regularly, is more powerful than anti-depressants. Building muscle strength by doing some weight-resistance training decreases the likelihood of dementia.

Diet – eat a well-balanced, nutrient-rich diet. Take a good quality multi-vitamin, especially if you eat a lot of processed foods. Eat foods that are rich in colour. Your body is very adept at eliminating toxins so simply de-toxify yourself by taking as many toxins out of your diet as possible.

Sleep – plan to get enough rest. It is one of the most powerful techniques of stress reduction. We live in a world that is sleep deprived, agitated and short-tempered. Refuse to join in. To sleep well you need to clear out your mind. A hour or so before you want to sleep lower the lights, write down any to-do items on a piece of paper so you don't need to keep them in mind overnight and also take some time to be grateful for the good things that have happened that day.

Sex – plan to have a great sex life. At times life is so busy and consuming, sex is the last thing on the agenda. Yet great sex is wonderful. It provides intimacy, love, closeness and it's good for your health as well. Planning time for and exploring different ways of having great sex is one of the finest quests in life. To be a great lover is a noble ambition.

Honour

This above all: to thine own self be true,
And it must follow, as the night the day,
Thou canst not then be false to any man.

William Shakespeare, *Hamlet*

Honour may seem like an old-fashioned concept. There are times when it feels in short supply in the modern world. Yet being honourable underpins many of the other essential aspects of life. Be true to your word. There is solidity and reliability in people who honour their own words, who do exactly what they say they will do.

The good opinion of others is desirable but being able to hold yourself and your own actions in high regard is essential for a great life. Acting with integrity, in accordance with your values is not always easy.

Choosing a few honourable role models and developing a code of conduct for yourself is a way of doing this. See if you can shape this into a daily reminder of who you want to be in the world.

One of the best examples I can think of comes from the work of John O'Donohue:

May I live this day
Compassionate of heart
Gentle in word,
Gracious in awareness
Courageous in thought
Generous in love.

Friendship and conversation

Friendship is the great connective thread that runs through our lives. It is the source of intimacy. It allows us to share our joys and our setbacks. Even the most passionate of romances will eventually dampen if not accompanied by friendship.

Cultivating the art of friendship and great conversation requires some thought and preparation. Too often conversation descends down to a trading of whose opinion is the correct one with an attack/defend pattern or an abrasion of egos.

Great conversations have more to do with curiosity than intellect or wit. We can prepare ourselves for great conversations by becoming informed not only about daily events but interesting facts or ideas, becoming intrigued by how other people think about these things and being prepared to ask them about their views and being prepared to give the conversation some priority.

We live in the age of distraction. Phones interrupt, text messages flow. Of course these are also other people wanting conversations.

A wonderful conversation is one of the most exhilarating and engrossing experiences we can have. For example, Einstein and a geologist friend were so engrossed by a discussion about earthquakes

'If I were reincarnated, I'd want to come back a buzzard. Nothing hates him or envies him or wants him or needs him. He is never bothered or in danger, and he can eat anything.' – William Faulkner, novelist

that neither noticed a big earthquake was happening and their building had been evacuated.

Humour

Developing an appreciation for the quirky, absurd, unpredictable, waywardness of human life is not only delightful it is also humbles us. It takes us back to our roots and grounds us.

The writer Douglas Adams once wrote, 'There is a theory which states that if ever anybody discovers exactly what the Universe is for and why it is here, it will instantly disappear and be replaced by something even more bizarre and inexplicable. There is another theory which states that this has already happened.'

> 'I spent a lot of money on booze, birds and fast cars. The rest I just squandered.' – George Best, soccer player

The world is so full of funny and inexplicable occurrences that it is hard not to think Douglas Adams was right. Laughter is the sound of freedom. It is the antidote to hubris and ego. Life is far too serious to be taken seriously.

Humour can contain within it great compassion for the dilemmas and perplexities that face us all. I am reminded of an old Marx Brothers movie in which Groucho plays a hotel manager and changes the numbers on all the rooms of the hotel. His staff protest, saying 'Think of the confusion it will cause.'

> 'If I had my life to live over again, I'd live over a saloon.'
> – W.C. Fields

'Yes,' replies Groucho, 'but think of all the fun.'

Music, dance and sounds

Rumi the poet said everything in the universe is a rhythmic drum beat, only love is the melody.

If the world comes close to a universal language, it is through music and dance. In his song 'Night and Day', Cole Porter incorporates the world of sound into music from the beat-beat of the tom-tom, the tick-tock of the stately clock and the drip-drip of raindrops. All the time we are surrounded by a world of rhythm and music and if we let it touch us and move us and sway us we are filled with harmonies and joy.

Aromas

One of the parts of you that develops first is your olfactory nerve and it links directly to the hippocampus in your brain where memories are stored. This is why certain smells may evoke long-forgotten memories. Aromas also play an important role in our enjoyment of food. About 75 per cent of the flavour we perceive in food comes from smelling it. There are also powerful associations between aromas and moods. We select the people we are attracted to based on their smell.

'Nothing is more important than this day.' – Goethe

Take time to absorb the aromas around you of baking bread, frangipani, ginger, sandalwood, eucalyptus, cedar, rosewater, lemon, or cinnamon and nutmeg.

Surround yourself with calming beautiful aromas that make your nostrils twitch with delight and make your heart soar.

Presence

Be everywhere you are. One of the most difficult things in our distracted, interrupted world is to, as spiritual leader Ram Dass would put it, be here now! To be truly present means clearing out your anticipations and your recollections and becoming open to what is happening ... right ... now.

Pause for a moment and do this. Make a practice of stopping several times a day and checking in with yourself and the immediate, present world around you. We live in a world that is future obsessed as we rush

> 'If I had my life over again I should form the habit of nightly composing myself to thoughts of death. I would practice, as it were, the remembrance of death. There is no other practice which so intensifies life. Death, when it approaches, ought not to take one by surprise. It should be part of the full expectancy of life. Without an ever-present sense of death life is insipid. You might as well live on the whites of eggs.'
> – Muriel Spark

towards the next thing. Occasionally we pause and become nostalgic. It's a shame that many of us don't seek happiness in the only place that it can exist: now.

Other cultures have conceptualised time differently. In some cultures time is treated as a universal present. For example, the Hopi Indians do not have a linear view of time.

There are times in our lives when attentive, aware immobility is helpful; a time to notice and watch rather than act. It may be useful to emulate the skill of an archer. Archery requires a steady hand and calm immobility. Highly skilled archers are said to try to release the arrow in the lull between heartbeats.

While long-term plans are useful, it is useful to learn how to slow down the pace of life, to make the most of each day and to enjoy the simple pleasures on offer in the present.

Former Beatle George Harrison was once asked what he had learned from his years of practising mediation and following Eastern philosophies. He responded by saying, 'I try to enjoy each and every moment.'

Spirituality

The multi-millionaire Kerry Packer was resuscitated after a major heart attack. After regaining consciousness he said, 'The good news is there's no devil. The bad news is there's no heaven. There's nothing there, do what you bloody well like.'

We can take Kerry's word that it is all a Godless empty existence, or instead we can think about the God that resides within all of us. How can we transform and nourish ourselves to be as God-like as possible? A deep sense of faith and spirituality allows us to dodge around the demands of our own ego and to connect with things much larger than ourselves.

All of the spiritual traditions contain great wisdom and converge at many points. There are two points in particular where they all agree. The first is to treat other people as you yourself would like to be treated. The second is to look beyond yourself, your day-to-day cares and worries, and to allow yourself to be transformed by finding your God.

Finding your God is one of the most important quests a human can place themselves upon. It is never frivolous and should not be dismissed with humour or trivialised. It is to be struck with awe at the power of nature, the sheer beauty of others, of forces beyond our own. Find your God in whatever form it is.

In the Western world that reveres the hamburger but neglects the animal whose life was taken to create it, that fears death but fails to consider the completion of a wonderful life, that applauds self-determination and rugged individualism and independence, seeking your own God may seem unfashionable. It takes an intense awareness of the world around us and deep questioning of the meaning of our existence. It takes times of reflection, reverence and ultimately reverie and bliss.

If I had my my life to live over

Someone asked me the other day if I had my life to live over, would I change anything.

My answer was no, but then I thought about it and changed my mind.

If I had my life to live over again I would have talked less and listened more.

Instead of wishing away nine months of pregnancy and complaining about the shadow over my feet, I'd have cherished every minute of it and realized that the wonderment growing inside me was to be my only chance in life to assist God in a miracle.

I would never have insisted the car windows be rolled up on a summer day because my hair had just been teased and sprayed.

I would have invited friends over to dinner even if the carpet was stained and the sofa faded.

I would have eaten popcorn in the 'good' living room and worried less about the dirt when you lit the fireplace.

I would have taken the time to listen to my grandfather ramble about his youth.

I would have burnt the pink candle that was sculptured like a rose before it melted in storage.

I would have sat cross-legged on the lawn with my children and never worried about grass stains.

I would have cried and laughed less while watching television ... and more while watching real life.

I would have shared more of the responsibility carried by my husband.

I would have eaten less cottage cheese and more ice cream.

I would have gone to bed when I was sick instead of pretending the Earth would go into a holding pattern if I weren't there for a day.

I would never have bought anything just because it was practical/wouldn't show soil/was guaranteed to last a lifetime.

When my child kissed me impetuously, I would never have said, 'Later, now go get washed up for dinner.'
There would have been more I love you's ... more I'm sorrys ... more I'm listening ...
But mostly, given another shot at life, I would seize every minute of it ... look at it and really see it ... try it on ... live it ... exhaust it ... and never give that minute back until there was nothing left of it.

Erma Bombeck

Beauty

Think about how lucky we are. All of the ancient civilisations have developed an aesthetic appreciation and have created and collected together beautiful art, gardens, sculptures and music. Walk along any street and look at the faces of people. Even those that are grim and drawn glow with beauty.

Take time to look at families of animals and the beauty of their interactions. To watch horses nuzzling on a misty morning or chimpanzees grooming one another, or birds courting and dancing in flight is to see a form of beauty that started long before we began and will continue long after we have gone.

Look at children playing, their faces filled with dreams and enthusiasm. As Neil Postman, the founder of the study of media studies once said, 'Children are the living messages we send to a time we ourselves will not see.'

All of that beauty available over all those centuries is available to us. Beauty represents the very best of humanity. We live in a time when all of the artworks in all of the galleries in the world are available for us to view at the touch of a button.

All of the beauty and wisdom available to Chaucer, Michelangelo, Da Vinci, Shakespeare, Mozart, Confucius, Marco Polo and Eleanor of

Aquitaine is available and accessible to you. Connecting with beauty and spirit puts us in touch with the eternals of humanity. It helps us to live broadly, richly and well. Meister Eckhart, a medieval philospher, once said, 'Time makes us old, Eternity keeps us young.'

Creativity

At many points throughout life, creativity is the doorway into a bigger and richer world. Creativity helps us to grow a life that is big enough for us to live in.

Creativity can be fostered and encouraged in ourselves. Building it means opening ourselves up to the outside influences of other people, art, dance, music, literature, plays and ideas. To be an avid participant in the pinnacles of human endeavour, creation and achievement is to truly live among the esteemed company of giants. Once you have supped at the fountain of greatness it is necessary to take time out from the cacophony of the world to listen your own inner voice and thoughts.

Sometimes we can work so hard, provide so much and be so busy we even lose sight of ourselves as creative people. That playful child that used to dream and make up stories and fantasies and at times lied through the back of her teeth has evaporated, leaving us to the desiccated life of adulthood. Dare to view yourself as creative. Play is the antidote to boredom.

Inspiration rarely comes without hard work. Just as a garden needs water, ideas need interest. Ideas regarded with interest grow and develop. Those ignored or treated with suspicion shrivel and die.

To accomplish this we need to develop an idea-capturing device, whether it be a journal, recorder or an art folio. Ideas and inspirations are slippery and unless taken hold of and recorded they can vanish.

We also need to learn how to pay close attention to dreams and sudden intuitions. Your unconscious is a faithful, diligent helper. Trust it with problems to solve and it will very often start giving you answers.

It is also great to develop crazy wisdom where you put together two or more seemingly incompatible ideas in nonsensical ways. Some combinations may be funny, or weird but by doing this we loosen up the fibres of imagination in our minds.

Love

Of all of the aspects of a great life, love is the most important. It is the song the universe sings to itself. Love is, as Leonard Cohen observed, the engine of survival.

While many spiritual and secular works speak of love, I feel I can do no better than to repeat the Bible from Corinthians, chapter 13 (Today's English Version):

> *I may be able to speak the languages of human beings and even of angels, but if I have no love, my speech is no more than a noisy gong or a clanging bell.*
>
> *I may have the gift of inspired preaching; I may have all knowledge and understand all secrets; I may have all the faith needed to move mountains – but if I have no love, I am nothing.*
>
> *I may give away everything I have, and even give up my body to be burned – but if I have no love, this does me no good.*
>
> *Love is patient and kind; it is not jealous or conceited or proud;*
>
> *Love is not ill-mannered or selfish or irritable; love does not keep a record of wrongs;*
>
> *Love is not happy with evil, but is happy with the truth.*
>
> *Love never gives up; and its faith, hope, and patience never fail.*
>
> *Love is eternal.*

Life

Life is precious and it is for living. A well-lived life reverberates with deep heartfelt intimacy. The sweet touch of a lover's embrace. The rambling conversations with friends, more like a song sung between people than a sharing of information where closeness is more important than content. The skipping, capering, playfulness of giddy-headedness. The giggling light-heartedness of laughter. The magic of nature with its turns and its rhythms and its changes. The heart-strung connections with loved ones that create webs of meaning. The delicate poetry of love. Music that resonates deep within you and sweeps you up to the pinnacles of delight. The nostril-twitching fragrance of food that speaks to you of home, time and love. The joy of discovery of new ideas, skills and ways of viewing life.

These are the treasures of life.

They can be buried by the rush of time, by the demands and the driven conquest of individual achievement. They can be over-looked or bought cheaply as imitations that fulfil desire for a moment but do not nourish you. They can, and will be, lost from sight in the dark alleyways of experience. The shadows of these times can burden us or help us to value the moments of light.

Of course, life also contains sorrows, loss, setbacks, challenges, pain, anguish, rejection and death. These are part of the journey we travel through. There is no need, however, to make them into permanent travel companions. Life is for living, and living life well is an improvisational art.

I hope that life does the same thing for you that springtime does for daffodils.

Appendix

The seven-year cycle

In many cultures the number seven is considered to have mystical qualities – the number that symbolises the relationship between humanity and the divine. Many religious followers believe the world was created in seven days, while there are seven days in the week, seven colours in a rainbow, seven musical notes, seven theological virtues and, of course, seven deadly sins. In the course of my research on the significance of the number seven in different religions I have drawn on numerous sources from the internet and recommend the following sites:

http://saptestele.wordpress.com/2010/07/28/the-magical-number-seven,
http://www.pbase.com/image/110107257,
http://en.wikipekia.org/wiki/7-(number)

Bahá'í

The mystical text *The Seven Valleys* by the Prophet-Founder Bahá'u'lláh relates the journey of the soul through the seven 'valleys' of Search, Love, Knowledge, Unity, Contentment, Wonderment and finally True Poverty and Absolute Nothingness.

Christianity

The number seven in the seven days of Creation is typological and also appears commonly throughout the Bible. For example:

- Seven days of Creation (Genesis 1).
- Seven years of plenty and seven years of famine in Pharaoh's dream (Genesis 41).
- Seven days of the feast of Passover (Exodus 13:3-10).

- Seven-day week and the pattern concerning distribution and use of manna (Exodus 16).
- Seven-year cycle around the years of Jubilee (Leviticus 25).
- The fall of the walls of Jericho on the seventh day after marching around the city seven times (Joshua 6).
- Seven things the Lord hates (Proverbs 6:16-19).
- Seven loaves multiplied into seven baskets of surplus (Matthew 15:32-37).
- The seven last words (or seven last sayings) of Jesus on the cross.
- Seven men of honest report, full of the Holy Ghost and wisdom (Acts 6:3).
- Seven Spirits of God are mentioned in the Book of Revelation.
- Seven churches of Asia to which the 'Book of Revelation' is addressed.
- Seven churches, seven stars, seven seals, seven last plagues, seven vials or bowls, seven thunders in the Revelation, the last book of the Bible.

Other descriptions of the number seven in Christian knowledge and practice include:

- The Seven Sacraments in the Catholic faith (though some traditions assign a different number).
- The Seven Joys of the Virgin Mary of Roman Catholic, Anglican, and other traditions.
- The Seven Sorrows of the Virgin Mary of Roman Catholic, Anglican, and other traditions.
- The Seven Corporal Acts of Mercy of Roman Catholic, Anglican, and other traditions.
- The Seven Spiritual Acts of Mercy of Roman Catholic, Anglican, and other traditions.

- The Seven Virtues: chastity, temperance, charity, diligence, kindness, patience and humility.
- The seven terraces of Mount Purgatory (one per deadly sin).

In the genealogy in the Gospel of Luke, Jesus is 77th in a direct line.

In the New Testament, the Gospel of Matthew 18:21, Jesus says to Peter to forgive seventy times seven.

There are seven suicides mentioned in the Bible (Old Testament and New Testament).

Hinduism

The Sanskrit word 'sapta' refers to number seven.

The Indian Music has 'sapta swaras', meaning seven octats (sa re ga ma pa dha ni), which are basics of music, from which hundreds of Ragas are composed.

Celestial group of seven stars are named as Sapta Rishi based on the seven great saints.

As per Hindu mythology, there are seven worlds in the universe, seven seas in the world and seven rishies (seven gurus) called sapta rishis.

There are seven Chakras.

Islam

There are seven heavens and Earths in Islamic tradition.

There are seven circumambulations (Tawaf) that are made around the Kaaba.

There are seven walks between Al-Safa and Al-Marwah mountains – that is travelling back and forth – seven times during the ritual pilgrimages of Hajj and Umrah.

There are seven fires in hell.

There are seven doors to heaven and hell.

Judaism

There are seven days of Passover and Sukkot when celebrated in Israel.

The menorah is a seven-branched candelabrum lit by olive oil in the tabernacle and the Temple in Jerusalem. The menorah is one of the oldest symbols of the Jewish people. It is said to symbolise the burning bush as seen by Moses on Mount Sinai (Exodus 25).

The number seven is a highly symbolic number in the Torah, alluding to the infusion of spirituality and Godliness into the creation. For example:

Genesis 2:3 – 'God rested on and sanctified the seventh day (Shabbat).'

A seven-day purification period is required for one who has become *tamei* to become *tahor*.

The *Shmita* (Sabbatical) year arrives every seventh year.

The Jubilee (*Yovel*) year comes after seven times seven years.

The Counting of the Omer leading up to the Giving of the Torah is expressed as '7 times 7 weeks'.

The weekly Torah portion is divided into seven *aliyahs*, and seven Jewish men (or boys over the age of thirteen who are considered men) are called up for the reading of these *aliyahs* during Shabbat morning services.

Seven blessings are recited under the *chuppah* during a Jewish wedding ceremony.

A Jewish bride and groom are feted with seven days of festive meals after their wedding, known as *Sheva Berachot* ('Seven Blessings').

The number of *Ushpizzin* (also known as the 'Seven Shepherds') who visit the *sukkah* during the holiday of Sukkot: Abraham, Isaac, Jacob, Joseph, Moses, Aaron and David.

The number of nations God told the Israelites they would displace when they entered the land of Israel (Deut. 7:1): the Hittite, the

Girgashite, the Amorite, the Canaanite, the Perizzite, the Hivite and the Jebusite.

In Breslov tradition, the seven orifices of the face (two eyes, two nostrils, two ears, and the mouth) are called The Seven Candles.

The number of times Cain will be avenged by God if he is murdered (Gen 4:15).

The Israelites circled Jericho for seven days and then the wall tumbled down.

Mythology

In Khasi mythology, the seven divine women who were left behind on earth and became the ancestresses of all humankind.

The number of gateways traversed by Inanna during her descent into the underworld.

The number of sleeping men in the Christian myth of the Seven Sleepers.

The Seven Sages in Sumerian mythology and various other mythologies.

The number of sages in Hindu mythology; their wives are the goddesses referred to as the Seven Mothers.

The number of main islands of mythological Atlantis.

In Guaraní mythology, the number of prominent legendary monsters.

Seven Lucky Gods exist in Japanese mythology.

In Irish mythology, the epic hero Cúchulainn is associated with the number seven. He has seven fingers on each hand, seven toes on each foot, and seven pupils in each eye.

In British folklore, every seven years the Fairy Queen pays a tithe to Hell in the tale of Tam Lin.

In the British folktale of *Thomas the Rhymer*, he went to live in the fairy kingdom for seven years.

The seven-branched sword in Korean mythology.

Others

According to some systems there are seven Archangels.

Seven is the minor symbol number of yang from the Taoist yin-yang.

There are seven palms in an Egyptian Sacred Cubit.

There are seven ranks in Mithraism.

The number seven is of particular significance within Cherokee cosmology.

In Buddhism, Buddha walked seven steps at his birth.

The holy scripture of the Moorish Science Temple of America is the Circle Seven Koran.

In Egypt cats are said to have seven lives as opposed to the Western culture legend of cats having nine lives.

The seventh glyph of the Mayan Calendar is Blue Hand. It represents the days in creation and is associated with creative perfection. This is the glyph of the last day of their calendar that ends on 21 December 2012.

References

Adler, A., (1927) *Understanding Human Nature*, Fawcett, London. This is Adler's masterpiece.

Anderson, J., (1999) *A Year by the Sea: Thoughts of an Unfinished Woman* Doubleday, New York.

Anderson J., (2006) *A Weekend to Change Your Life: Find Your Authentic Self After a Lifetime of Being All Things to All People*, Broadway Books, New York. Joan Anderson writes beautifully about re-connecting with herself by using the ebbing tide as a metaphor for her own need to retreat before renewing.

Baker, J., (1982) *Tolstoy's Bicycle: Who Did What When?* Panther, London. A marvellous compendium of the age people accomplished things in their lives.

Baniel, A., (2009) *Move Into Life: The Nine Essentials for Lifelong Vitality*, Harmony Books, New York. Anat Baniel integrates the research on neuroplasticity with the need to build strength, flexibility and muscle power.

Bateson, M.C., (1990) *Composing A Life*, Plume, New York. Mary Bateson's beautiful review of the pivotal moments in women's lives.

Booker, C., (2004) *The Seven Basic Plots: Why We Tell Stories*, Continuum, New York. Christopher Booker's fascinating book covers stories and why we tell them as well as what they mean for us. A truly monumental book that took 26 years to research and write. It is an inspirational triumph.

Bridges, W., (2004) *Transitions: Making Sense of Life's Changes*, Perseus Books, Cambridge. William was one of the pioneers in the area of life transitions.

Chodron, P., (2000) *When Things Fall Apart: Heart Advice for Difficult Times*, Shambala, Boston. Pema Chodron's remarkable book talks of how to create compassion and wisdom out of hard times.

Claxton, E. (Ed), (2005) *The Book of Life: A Compendium of the Best Autobiographical and Memoir Writing*, Random House, London. What a collection of gems!

Cohen, G.D., (2000) *The Creative Age: Awakening Human Potential in the Second Half of Life*, Quill, New York.

Csikszentmihalyi, M., (1990) *Flow: The Psychology of Happiness*, Rider Press, London.

Csikszentmihalyi, M., (1996) *Creativity*, Harper, New York. Mihalyi Csikszentmihalyi's fantastic books should be essential reading for anyone wanting to make the most of their life.

Dass, R., (1971) *Remember: Be Here Now*, Hanuman Foundation, New York.

Earnshaw, A., (1998) *Time Bombs in Families and How to Survive Them*, Spencer, Melbourne. A sadly little known gem that talks about the echoes and resonances in family patterns.

Erikson, E.H., (1980) *Identity and the Life Cycle*, Norton and Company, New York.

Erikson, E.H., (1997) *The Life Cycle Completed:* (Extended Version), Norton and Company, New York.

Erikson, J.M., (1988) *Wisdom and the Senses: The Way of Creativity*, Norton and Company, New York. Erik and Joan Erickson were pioneers and inspirers of all who consider adult human development. They influenced Joan Andersen, William Bridges, Daniel Levinson, Gail Sheehy and definitely myself.

Fraiberg, S.H., (1959) *The Magic Years: Understanding and Handling the Problems of Early Childhood*, Simon and Schuster, New York. Shiela Fraiberg's book remains the best book I have ever read on early childhood.

Frankl, V., (1946) *Man's Search for Meaning*

Friday, N., (1977) *My Mother Myself*, Fontana/Collins, New York.

Friedan, B., (1993) *The Fountain of Age*, Simon and Schuster, New York.
Gallway, T.W., (1976) *The Inner Game of Tennis: The Classic Guide to the Mental Side of Peak Performance*.
Gerzon, M., (1992) *Listening to Midlife: Turning Your Crisis into a Quest*, Shambala, Boston.
Golas, T., (1971) *The Lazy Man's Guide to Enlightenment*, Seed, Palo Alto. Thaddeus Golas's wise book includes concepts of life and awareness expanding as well as the idea that they only failure we ever have in life is the failure to love enough.
Gopnik, A., Meltzoff, A. and Kuhl, P., (1999) *How Babies Think*, Weidenfeld and Nicolson, London. Alison Gopnik and her colleagues sit beside Shiela Fraiberg as the most complete chroniclers of infancy and childhood.
Hawes, M., (2006) *Twenty Good Summers*, Allen and Unwin, Crows Nest. Martin Hawes's book provides a well-thought-out method of making the most of your life and your finances in the senior years of life.
Hillman, J., (1997) *The Soul's Code: In Search of Character and Calling*, Grand Central Publishing, New York. James Hillman has a lovely outline of the power that destiny plays in our lives.
Hudson, F.M. and McLean, P.D (2006) *Lifelaunch: A Passionate Guide to the Rest of Your Life*, Hudson, Santa Barbara. Frederic Hudson and Pamela McLean's book is a great outline of how to create a pathway of renewal in your life and to put in place the stepping stones towards vitality.
Johnson, R., (1991) *Transformation: Understanding the Three Levels of Masculine Consciousness*, Harper Collins, New York. Robert Johnson described this to me as his best book. In an unpublished talk titled 'The transitions of life', Robert spoke about the seven-year cycle and, without doubt, was one of the most important inspirations for this book.
Jung, C., (1933) *Modern Man in Search of a Soul*, Harvest, San Diego.

Kessel, B., (2008) *It's Not about the Money: A Financial Game Plan for Staying Safe, Sane and Calm in Any Economy,* Harper One, New York. Brent Kessel's examination of the restless wanting mind and how to quieten it so that we are not destined to be ever discontented is a fantastic contribution.

Kopp, S., (1976) *If You Meet Buddha On The Road, Kill him!* Bantam Books, New York. Sheldon Kopp wrote so many inspirational books that brought together vast amounts of knowledge from other cultures as well as his own clinical and life lessons.

Langer, E.J., (2009) *Counter Clockwise: Mindful Health and the Power of Possibility,* Ballantine Books, New York. Ellen Langer's books on mindfulness teach how to make the most of presence.

Levinson, D., (1978) *The Seasons of a Man's Life,* Ballantine, New York.

Levinson, D., (1996) *The Seasons of a Woman's Life,* Ballantine, New York. Daniel Levinson was a remarkable man who gathered together the stories and patterns of people's lives. Gail Sheehy in her series *Passages and Pathways* acknowledges her use of Daniel's work.

Livingstone, G., (2005) *Too Soon Old, Too late Smart: Thirty things you need to know now,* Hodder, Sydney. Gordon Livingston's wise erudite account of what is truly important in life.

Moody, H.R. and Carroll, D., (1998) *The Five Stages of the Soul: Charting the Spiritual Passages That Shape Our Lives,* Anchor, New York. A beautiful evocation of the spiritual development that occurs throughout adult hood. Delightfully wise.

O'Connor, P., (1981) *Understanding the Mid-life Crisis,* MacMillan, Sydney.

O'Connor, P., (2000) *Facing the fifties: From Denial to Reflection,* Allen and Unwin, Crows Nest. Peter O'Connor is a wise Jungian analyst who writes beautifully and sagely about the twists and turns of the inner world.

O'Donohue, J., (2005) *Beauty: The invisible embrace*, Harper Perennial, New York. When John O'Donohue died in 2008, the world lost a wonderful poet, thinker and wise man.

Sampson, A. and Sampson, S., (1985) *The Oxford Book of Ages*, Oxford University Press, Oxford.

Schachter-Shalomi, Z. and Miller, R.S., (1995) *From Age-ing to Sage-ing: A Profound New Vision of Growing Older*, Grand Central Publishing, New York. A really positive way of viewing the senior years and the contribution that can be made in life.

Sharples, R., (2006) *Meditation and Relaxation in Plain English*, Wisdom Publications, Boston. Bob Sharples has been an inspiration and friend to me and was integral to the creation of this book. Without my conversations with Bob this book could never have been written.

Sheehy, G., (1981) *Pathfinders*, William Morrow and Co., New York.

Sheehy, G., (1984) *Passages: Predictable crisis of Adult Life*, Bantam Books, New York.

Sheehy, G., (1998) *The Silent Passage*: Revised and updated edition, Pocket Books, New York.

Sheehy, G., (1999) *Understanding Men's Passages: Discovering the New Map of Men's Lives*, Ballantine, New York. Gail Sheehy's wonderful contribution to the understanding of adult development has been nothing less than phenomenal.

Sher, B., (1979) *Wishcraft: How to get what you really want*, Ballantine Books, New York.

Vailliant, G., (2002) *Ageing Well: Surprising Guideposts to a Happier Life From the Landmark Harvard Study of Adult Development*, Scribe, Melbourne.

Vittachi, N., (2000) *The Feng Shui Detective*, Duffy and Snellgrove, Sydney. Such a lot of wisdom disguised as great fun!

Whyte, D., (2002) *Crossing the Unknown Sea*, Riverhead Trade, London. David Whyte's poetry and talks have been an inspirational force in my own life and his provides a beacon of wisdom in a fraught world of much information but little knowledge.

Young-Eisendrath, P., (2000) *Women and Desire: Beyond Wanting to be Wanted,* Piaktkus, London.

Yun, H., (2005), *Tending Life's Garden: Between Ignorance and Enlightenment V1,* Buddha's Light Publishing, California.

Zeldin, T., (1994) *An intimate history of humanity,* Harper Collins, New York.

Zeldin, T., (1998) *Conversation: How Talk can Change our Lives,* Hidden Spring, New Jersey. Theodare Zeldin's historical accounts of the power of change in life and the essence of great conversations is stunning.

Author Notes

Page iv **'It's almost as if we reinvent who we are every seven years.'** Obviously in a lifespan many things happen, so while the seven-year cycle provides a useful map it will not fit every person, culture or situation. Nevertheless, it is a useful beginning point and even if your life is at variance with this pattern I hope it will provide you with food for thought and conversation.

Page ix **'Shakespeare wrote in *As You Like It* ...'** William Shakespeare, *As You Like It*, (II. 7).

Page xi **'While there are varying opinions about the names and timings of the phases ...'** There is general agreement that life goes through stages. Renown psychologist Daniel Levinson identified six stages, each overlapping to some degree: childhood 0–22, early adult transition 17–22, early adulthood 17–45, mid-life transition 40–45, middle adulthood 40–65. Late adulthood starts at about 60. Erik Erickson in *Childhood and Society* (1950) spoke of eight ego stages. The first five cover infancy through to adolescence. Stage six is intimacy versus isolation and this begins at the beginning of young adulthood, age 20. Stage eight, integrity or despair, accompanies old age from 60 onwards. Jose Ortega Y Gasset, author of *Man and Crisis* (1933) identified five main stages: childhood 0–15, youth 15–30, initiation 30–45, dominant 45–60 and old age 60+.

Page x **'You start out dead ...'** This has also been attributed to George Carlin. For more see <http://dossierjournal.com/news/and-you-finish-off-as-an-orgasm/>

Page xi **'I don't want to achieve immortality ...'** Woody Allen, see <http://www.quotationspage.com/quote/52.html>

Page xi **'... which are ideas and concepts that have evolved over human history ...'** Carl Jung thought personality development did not progress very far beyond adolescence but dealt mainly during the twenties and thirties with material repressed during childhood (known as the shadow).

Page xiv '**One example of recurring theme is that over 1000 variations ...**' Sir James Fraser shows in *The Golden Bough* (1890) that there are remarkable similarities between myths and folktales of the entire world such as the God who dies and is reborn.

Page 1 '**... For the straightforward pathway had been lost.**' Dante Alighieri, 'The Divine Comedy'. Dante Alighieri (1265–1321) is considered one of Italy's greatest poets. He wrote 'The Divine Comedy' over a period of 12 years, completing the work the year before he died. In 'The Divine Comedy' Dante takes us through Hell (Inferno), Purgatory (Purgatorio), and then reaches Heaven (Paradiso). His journey serves as an allegory of the progression of the individual soul toward God.

Page 3 '**There is a tide in the affairs of men ...**' William Shakespeare, *Julius Caesar* (IV. 3.2-81).

Page 5 '**The many bends along the highroad of my life ...**' *Power of a Woman: Memoirs of a turbulent life, Eleanor of Acquitaine*, Robert Fripp, Shillingstone Press, Toronto, 2006.

Page 6 '**Don't weep for like a woman ...**' was said by Sultana Ayelsha, mother of Boabdil (Abu-Abdallah), the last king of Granada. *Time* magazine, January 13, 1986. For more see <http://www.time.com/time/magazine/article/0,9171,1074911-3,00.html>

Page 11 '**Fans, for the past two weeks ...**' Lou Gehrig's speech can be found at <http://www.lougehrig.com/about/speech.htm>

Page 11 '**For Mother Teresa, 'It was a command I had to obey.'** See <http://www.vatican.va/news_services/liturgy/saints/ns_lit_doc_20031019_madre-teresa_en.html>

Page 12 '**At the age of thirty-eight Jean Paul Sartre wrote ...**' <http://mms-humanities.wikispaces.com/Jean-Paul+Sartre>

Page 14 '**Gertrude Stein, upon hearing of the freakish death commented dryly ...' See <http://www.goodreads.com/author/quotes/9325.Gertrude_Stein->

Page 17 'Echoing thoughts similar to the Buddha's, Socrates is reported to have commented that ...' See <http://www.2020site.org/socrates/personalcharacteristics.html>

Page 18 'The seventieth birthday ...' Mark Twain's speech is available from <http://www.write-out-loud.com/mark-twains-70th-birthday-speech.html>

Page 19 'As Crowfoot (1821–1890), the Blackfoot Native American observed, 'What is life? ...' See <http://www.quoteworld.org/quotes/3295>

Page 20 'Ignoring these patterns condemns people ...' from *The Great Gatsby*, F. Scott Fitzgerald, Scribner, New York, 1925.

Page 25 'This is also known as mindfulness.' I am grateful to Timothy Gallwey for the concept of the true and critical self and to Bob Sharples who taught me so much about mindfulness and has been a key inspiration for this book.

Page 25 'There are many places of power in the world ...' I am grateful to the work of John O'Donohue who made this point.

Page 26 'I think the splendor of my childhood ...' This is taken from *Before Night Falls: A Memoir* by Reinaldo Arenas, translated by Delores. M. Koch, Penguin, 1994. Copyright 1993 by the estate of Reinaldo Arenas, translation by Delores. M. Koch. Reprinted by permission of Viking Penguin, a division of Penguin Books (USA) Inc. Found in Eve Claxton (Ed.) *The book of Life: A compendium of the best autobiographical and memoir writing* Ebury Press (Random House), London, 2005.

Page 27 'Babies can't design a continuous ...' *How Babies Think: The science of childhood*, Alison Gopnik, Andrew Meltzoff and Patricia Kuhl, Weidenfeld and Nicolson, London, 1999.

Page 30 '... many children are mistresses or masters of the universe ...' The point is beautifully elucidated by Sheila Fraiberg.

Page 30 'A. A. Milne beautifully stated this in the first stanza of his poem 'Disobedience' ...' 'Disobedience', AA Milne, cannot find direct source.

Page 32 'It is a hot day...' *The Feng Shui Detective*, Nury Vittachi, Allen & Unwin, Sydney, 2008. Reprinted with kind permission of Allen & Unwin.

Page 36 'Seven years and six months!' *Alice in Wonderland*, C.S. Lewis, 1865.

Page 39 'There is a strong history of successful people who did poorly at school.' For more see <http://avinashgamerboy.artician.com/blog/2009/09/famous-people-who-failed-but-succeeded/>

Page 40 'Seven to eleven is a huge chunk of life...' See<http://www.iwise.com/xKskw>

Page 41 'So the playground was hell...' Taken from *Bad Blood: A Memoir*, Lorna Sage, Fourth Estate, London, 2000, reprinted with kind permission of HarperCollins.

Page 44 'I had arrived at that difficult and unattractive age ...' This is taken from *My Autobiography*, Charles Chaplin, Bodley Head, 1964. Reprinted by permission of Random House in Eve Claxton (Ed.) *The book of Life: A compendium of the best autobiographical and memoir writing*, Ebury Press, Random House, London, 2005.

Page 49 'As Robert Bly puts it ...' *Iron John: A Book About Men*, Robert Bly, De Capo Press, USA, 2004.

Page 51 'School was all wrong ...' *Harpo Speaks!* Harpo Marx with Rowland Barber, Vicotr Gollancz, London, 1961. Reprinted by permission of Amadeus Press/Limelight Editions.

Page 56 'The day after graduating ...' *Something for Everyone*, David Sedaris, Little, Brown and Co., New York, 1997. Reproduced with kind permission.

Page 57 'The art is to develop self-confidence without arrogance.' The power of male role models is well recognised in literature and Life. Dante had Virgil to guide him through the underworld, Arthur had Merlin, Frodo had Gandalf, Odysseus had Teiresias to instruct him about what he needs to do to return to Ithaca and Harry Potter had Professor Dumbledore.

The feminine counterparts include Athene the goddess of wisdom, Galadriel in *Lord of the Rings* and Beatrice in Dante's *Comedia,* all of whom personify grace, beauty, and the ability to see the whole.

Page 59 **'There are four main ways that people do the work of identity formation.'** The four main ways of attaining identity formation is derived from the work of James Marcia.

Page 60 **'Let not young souls ...'** Vachel Lindsay, *The Congo and Other Poems*, Bibliolife, USA, 2008.

Page 62 **'The Johari window provides ...'** The Johari window was created by Joseph Luft and Harry Ingham in 1955 and is called the 'Johari' window because it is a combination of their names, Joe and Harry.

Page 64 **'This book has a big enough task trying to cover** human life without adding dream analysis to its contents ...' I am grateful to Robert Johnson for teaching me about the meanings of dreams.

Page 64 **'As the poet David Whyte notes ...'** The talks and poetry of David Whyte have been inspirational to me. For more go to <http//:www.davidwhyte.com>

Page 65 **'There is a vitality, a life force ...'** Agnes DeMille, *Martha: The Life and Work of Martha Graham*, Knopf Doubleday Publishing Group, USA, 1992.

Page 71 **'... give up what needs to be given up ...'** *The Five Stages of the Soul: Charting the Spiritual Passages That Shape Our Lives*, Hank Moody and David Caroll, Anchor, New York. 1998. Reproduced with kind permission by Random House.

Page 74 *The Inner Game of Tennis: The Classic Side to The Mental Side of Peak Performance*, W. Timothy Gallwey, Random House, USA, 1974.

If You Meet the Buddha on the Road, Kill Him! The Pilgrimage of Psychotherapy Patients by Sheldon B. Kopp, Bantam Books, 1976.

Strengths Finder 2.0: A New and Updated Edition of the Online Test from Gallup's Now, Discover Your Strengths, Tom Rath, Gallop Press, USA, 2007.

What Colour is Your Parachute? A Practical Manual for Job-Hunters and Career-Changers, Richard N. Bolles, Ten Speed Press, North America, 2004.

Wishcraft: How to Get What You Really Want by Barbara Sher and Annie Gottlieb, Ballantine Books, 2003.

Page 78, '**To a Mouse**', *Selected Poems of Robert Burns,* Carol McGirk, Penguin Classics, UK, 1993, p. 67. The original line is 'The best laid schemes o' Mice an' Men'.

Page 79 I am grateful for an unpublished talk given by Robert Johnson titled 'The Transformations of Life'. This talk was not only the source of the information about guardian angels but served as an initial inspiration for this book.

Page 87 *Flow: The psychology of happiness*, M. Csikszentmihalyi, Rider Press, London, 1990.

Meditation and Relaxation in Plain English, Bob Sharples, Wisdom Publications, MA, USA, 2006.

Page 90 The Chinese fable of the stonecutter is adapted from <http://www.aikidoki.net/SOULFOOD/stories.htm>

Page 93 This extract is taken from a speech given by Robert Kennedy at the University of Kansas in 1968. See <http://www.mccombs.utexas.edu/faculty/michael.brandl/main%20page%20items/Kennedy%20on%20GNP.htm>

Page 98 Placing an asterisk next to the age your same-sex parent when they had the next child in your family comes directly from the work of Averil Earnshaw. See *Time Bombs in Families and How to Survive Them*, Averil Earnshaw, Spencer, Melbourne, 1998.

Page 100 '**I had, I suppose ...**' *Clinging to the Wreckage: A Part of Life*, John Mortimer, Penguin, UK, 1983. Reproduced with kind permission.

Page 101 *Too Soon Old, Too Late Smart – Thirty Things You Need to Know Now*, G. Livingstone, Hodder, Sydney, 2005.

Page 112, 'Résumé', *Enough Rope*, Dorothy Parker, 1926.

Page 112 **'Your basic extended family...'** *Funny Sauce*, Delia Ephron, Signet, Penguin, NY, 1988. Reprinted with kind permission of Viking Penguin, a division of Penguin Group (USA) Inc.

Page 113 The point is made powerfully by the poet David Whyte, when he says the answer to exhaustion is not always rest, it is wholeheartedness. See *Crossing the Unknown Sea: work as a pilgrimage of identity*, Riverhead, New York, 2001. For more go to <http://www.davidwhyte.com/crossing.htm>

Page 114 **'Why are you so unhappy? ...'** *Ask the Awakened: The Negative Way*, Wei Wu Wei, Routledge and Kegan Paul Ltd, London, 2002.

Page 114 **'Thoroughly unprepared ... '** Carl Jung as cited from http://www.goodreads.com/quotes/show/131993.

Page 116 Inscription on the tomb on an Anglican Bishop taken from<http://robbinquotes.blogspot.com/2007/01/inscription-on-tomb-of-anglican-bishop.html>

Page 119 *It's Not about the money: a financial game plan for staying safe, sane and calm in any economy,* Brent Kessel, Harper One, New York, 2008.

First Things First, Stephen Covey, A. Roger Merrill and R. Merrill, Fireside, New York, 1994.

The E-Myth Revisited: Why Most Small Businesses Don't Work and What to Do About It, Michael E. Gerber, Harper Business New York, 1995.

Facing the Fifties: From Denial To Reflection, Peter O' Connor, Allen and Unwin, Sydney, 2000.

Page 123 *The Rites of Passage,* Arnold Van Gennep, Routledge, 1909.

Page 129 **'Joan Andersen writes ...'** *A Weekend to Change Your Life: Find Your Authentic Self After a Lifetime of Being All Things to All People*, Joan Anderson, Broadway Books, New York, 2006.

Page 133 *Twenty Good Summers*, Martin Hawes, Allen and Unwin, Sydney, 2006.

Lifelaunch: A passionate guide to the rest of your life, Frederic Hudson and Pamela McLean, Hudson PR, Santa Barbara, 2006.

Crossing the Unknown Sea, David Whyte, Riverhead Trade, London, 2002.

Page 136 **'Thaddeus Golas in his wise book ...'** *The Lazy Man's Guide to Enlightenment*, T. Golas, Seed, Palo Alto, 1971.

Page 136 **'This dive for the eiderdown of comfort ...'** The tree of Idleness at Bellapias is described in *Bitter Lemons*, Laurence Durrell, Faber and Faber, London, 1957.

Page 137 **'As Martin Hawes comments ...'** *Twenty Good Summers*, Martin Hawes, Allen and Unwin, Sydney, 2006.

Page 138 **'As Howard Thurman, American theologian ...'** See Howard Thurman <http://thinkexist.com/quotes/howard_thurman/>

Page 139 **'Mythologist Joseph Campbell points out ...'** see Joseph Campbell, <http://www.philosophersnotes.com/quotes/by_teacher/Joseph+Campbell/page/3>

Page 144 **'Luke Rhinehart ...'** *The Dice Man*, Luke Rhinehart, Woodstock, New York, 2001.

Page 145 Ithaka poem by C.P. Cavafy, taken from *C.P. Cavafy: Collected Poems*. (Revised ed.) C.P. Cavafy, edited by George Savidis, translated by Edmund Keeley and Philip Sherrar, Princeton Press, USA, 1992. Reproduced with kind permission by Princeton Press.

Page 147 *Ageing well: Surprising guideposts to a happier life from the Landmark Harvard Study of Adult Development*, George Vailliant, Scribe, Melbourne, 2002.

Transformations: Understanding the Three Levels of Masculinity, Robert Johnson, HarperCollins, USA, 1993.

Page 153 **'As Joan Anderson says ...'**, *A Weekend to Change Your Life: Find Your Authentic Self After a Lifetime of Being All Things to All People*, J. Anderson, Broadway Books, New York, 2006.

Page 153 *The Jumping Jeweller of Lavendar Bay* by Hugh Atkison, 1992, Viking, Melbourne, then popularised in song by the Little River Band.

Page 154 **'When Death Comes'**, Mary Oliver, is from *New and Selected Poems by Mary Oliver*, Beacon Press, Boston, MA, 1992. Reproduced with kind permission by Beacan Press.

Page 157 *Zorba the Greek*, N. Kazantakis, Simon and Schuster, New York, 1952.

The Five Stages of the Soul: charting the spiritual passages that shape our lives, H.R. Moody, and D. Carroll, Anchor, New York, 1998.

From Age-ing to Sage-ing: A profound new vision of growing older, Z. Schachter-Shalomi, and R.S. Miller, Grand Central Publishing, New York, 1995.

Page 160 **'About this issue of ageing ...'**, Doris Lessing, from *Women turning 70: Honoring the Voices of Wisdom* by Cathleen Rountree, Jossey-Bass, 1999.

Page 161 **Interview with Li Ching Yuen**, 'Tortoise-Pigeon-Dog' from *Time* magazine, May 15, 1933.

Page 162 Sheldon Kopp's Escatological Laundry List is reproduced with permission from *If You Meet Buddha on the Side of the Road, Kill Him!*, Science and Behaviour Books, California.

Page 166 **'When you are in your middle seventies ...'** P.G. Wodehouse, *Over Seventy: An Autobiography With Digressions*, 1957, reproduced with permission from Eve Claxton (Ed.) *The Book of Life: A Compendium of the Best Autobiographical and Memoir Writing*, Ebury Press, Random House, London, 2005.

Page 167 *Beauty the Invisible Embrace*, John O' Donohue, HarperCollins, New York, 2005.

Conversation: How Talk Can Change Our Lives, Theodore Zeldin, The Harville Press, London, 1998.

Page 169 **'I have reigned more than fifty years ...'** Abd-ar-Raham III. See <http://www.allaboutphilosophy.org/abd-ar-rahman-iii.htm> Reproduced with permission from www.allaboutphilosophy.org

– published by AllAboutGOD.com Ministries, M. Houdmann, P. Matthews-Rose, R. Niles, editors, 2002–2010.

Page 174 'On my last birthday ... ', *Joys and Sorrows, Reflections*, Pablo Casals, HarperCollins, 1970.

Page 176 'Death stands above me whispering low I know ...' Cited from <http://quotes.dictionary.com/Death_stands_above_me_whispering_low_I_know.

Page 177 'Do not stand at my grave and weep ...' Cited from <http://www.poetrylibrary.org.uk/queries/faps/#5>

Page 178 *A Move Into Life: The Nine Essentials for Lifelong Vitality*, A. Baniel, Harmony Books, New York, 2009.

When Things Fall Apart: Heart Advice For Difficult Times, P. Chodron, Shambala, Boston, 2000.

Page 181 'It's such a little thing to weep ...' Emily Dickinson (1830–1886) For more information go to <http://www.love-poetry-of-the-world.com/famous-love-poetry-emily-dickinson1.html>

Page 182 'Evariste Galois, mathematical genius ...' There is some debate about how much of his theory was completed on the last night of his life but there is little doubt that he outlined it in frenzied letters to his friends at that time. For more go to <http://www.galois-group.net/>

Page 182 'My little wife Ila and Borsi ...' Ganier Raymond, Philippe, 1975, L'affiche rouge / Philippe Ganier Raymond Fayard, Paris, Glasz Imre letter, accessed February 2010 from <http://marxists.anu.edu.au/history/france/resistance/manouchian/letters/glasz.htm>

Page 183 '... to a condition of complete simplicity costing not more than everything.' This line is taken from the poem *Four Quartets, Little Gidding*, by T.S. Elliot.

Page 184 'There is an old Sufi story ...' *The Exploits of the Incomparable Mulla Nasrudin: The Subtleties of the Inimitable Mulla Nasrudin*, Idries Shah, Octagon Press, London, 1989. Mulla Nasrudin http://www.nasruddin.org/

Page 186 **The Ravensbruck prayer**, *The Oxford Book of Prayer*, Oxford University Press, USA, 2002; or see <http://oblations.blogspot.com/2008/06/ravensbruck-prayer.html>

Page 186 **'If you go back ten generations ...'** Calculated by O. Hooge, BC, Canada. For more go to <http://members.shaw.ca/tfrisen/chances_of_you_existing.htm>

Page 187 *Notes from a Small Island*, Bill Bryson, Doubleday, London, 1995.

Page 189 **'May I live this day ...'** *Eternal Echoes: Exploring our Yearning to Belong,* John O'Donohue, New York, 1999. Reproduced with kind permission of Random House and The John O'Donohue Estate.

Page 190 **'The writer Douglas Adams once wrote ...'** The Restaurant at the End of the Universe, *The Ultimate Hitchhikers Guide to the Galaxy*, Douglas Adams, Random House, USA, 1999. Reproduced with kind permission.

Page 192, **'If I had my life over again I should form the habit of nightly composing myself to thoughts of death ...'** *Momento Mori*, Muriel Spark, New Directions Publishing, 2000. Reproduced with kind permission of New Directions Publishing.

Page 192 **'The multi-millionaire Kerry Packer ...'** See http://news.ninemsn.com.au/article.aspx?id=79011

Page 193 **'If I had my life to life over'** by Erma Bombeck, reproduced with permission from the Aaron M. Priest Literary Agency.

Page 195 **'As Neil Postman, founder of media studies ...'** For more go to <http://www.flakmag.com/opinion/postman.html>

Page 196 Meister Eckhardt was a 14th century theologian, philosopher and mystic. For more go to <http://www.eckhartsociety.org/>

Permissions

Every effort has been made to source and seek permission from the last known copyright holder for all the quotes and extracts used in this text.

The extract on page 26 is from 'The Grove', *Before Night Falls: A Memoir* by Reinaldo Arenas, translated by Dolores M. Koch, ©1993 by the Estate of Reinaldo Arenas and Dolores M. Koch. Used by permission of Viking Penguin, a division of Penguin Group (USA) Inc.

The extract on page 32 is from *The Feng Shui Detective* by Nury Vittachi, Allen & Unwin, Sydney, 2008, and is reproduced with permission by Allen & Unwin.

The extract on page 41 is from *Bad Blood: A Memoir* by Lorna Sage, © 2000 by Lorna Sage, reproduced with permission by HarperCollins Publishers, USA.

The quote on page 44 is from *My Autobiography*, Charles Chaplin, Bodley Head, 1964. Reprinted by permission of Random House in Eve Claxton 2005 (Ed.), *The Book of Life: A Compendium of the Best Autobiographical and Memoir Writing,* Ebury Press, Random House, London.

The extract on page 51 is taken from *Harpo Speaks!* by Harpo Marx and Rowland Barber, ©1962 Harpo Marx and Rowland Barber, reproduced with permission from Hal Leonard Corporation.

The extract on page 56 is from 'Something For Everyone', *Naked* by David Sedaris, Little, Brown and Co., New York, 1997. Reproduced with permission of Don Congdon Associates, Inc. © 1997 by David Sedaris.

The extract on page 100 is from *Clinging to the Wreckage: A Part of Life*, John Mortimer, Penguin, UK, 1983. Reproduced with kind permission of Penguin Books Ltd © Advan Press Ltd, 1982.

The extract on page 112 is from *Funny Sauce* by Delia Ephron ©1982,1983,1986 by Delia Ephron. Reproduced with permission of Viking Penguin, a division of Penguin Group (USA) Inc.

The poem on page 145 is taken from *C.P. Cavafy* by Edmund Keeley, ©1975 by Edmund Keeley and Philip Sherrard. Reproduced with permission of Princeton University Press.

The poem on page 154 'When Death Comes' is by Mary Oliver from *New and Selected Poems: Volume One*, copyright © 1992 Mary Oliver and is reproduced with permission by Beacon Press, Boston.

The quote on page 166 is from *Over Seventy*, P.G. Wodehouse, 1957. Reproduced by permission of Random House in Eve Claxton 2005 (Ed.) *The Book of Life: A Compendium of the Best Autobiographical and Memoir Writing* Ebury Press (Random House) London.

The quote on page 176 from Arthur Miller is taken from *Timebends: A life* by Arthur Miller, Penguin, 1995. Reproduced with permission from Grove/Atlantic New York.

The quote on page 189 is from *Bless this Space: A Book of Blessings* by John O'Donohue, copyright © 2008 by John O'Donohue. Reprinted with permission of Doubleday, a division of Random House, Inc, and the John O'Donohue Estate.

The extract on page 192 is from *Momento Mori* by Muriel Spark, New Directions Publishing Corporation, 2000. Reproduced with permission of New Directions Publishing Corporation.

The extract on page 193 is by Erma Bombeck and is reproduced with permission by The Aaron M. Priest Literary Agency.

Acknowledgements

There are so many people who have contributed to this book. Their perspectives, ideas and willingness to share thoughts and generosity is overwhelming.

I am deeply grateful to you all.

Particular thanks to Jen Aldridge, Lyn Amy, Julie Barclay, Anthony Beardall, Bob Bellhouse, Noel Cranswick, Lorraine Day, Mary Duma, Rod Dungan, Rex Finch, Vicki Fuller, Lucy Fuller, Sam Fuller, Richard Fuller, Brenda Hosking-Brown, Luis Huck, Rodney Knight, Ola Krupinska, Nell Jones, Paul Jones, Ian Larsen, Karen McGraw, Rob McNeilly, Sam Miles, Chris Miller, Esme Murphy, John Nicholas, Georgie Nutton, Ric Pawsey, Ken Robinson, Bob Sharples, Robert Schweitzer, Michael Schwarz, Meredith Shears, Michele Silva, Trish Steele, Jim Twomey, David Tyson, Barbara Watterston, Peter Wicking, Peter Wiltshire, Digby Williamson, Kerry Winchester and Wilma Wolter.

Thank you to my teachers. You have given me a gift that I will spend the rest of my life unwrapping.

Other Finch books of interest

A Language Older Than Words
Derrick Jensen

In this powerful mix of memoir and environmental expose, Jensen depicts our civilisation's core dissonance. His portrayal of our industrial economy's abuse of our environment, destruction of meaningful work, disconnection from the natural world and indifference towards healthy relationships is masterfully contrasted with his personal attempt to live in harmony with non-human life.
ISBN 978 1876451 950

Nature and the Human Soul
A road map to discovering our place in the world
Bill Plotkin

Given the perilous state of our planet's environment, Bill Plotkin (wilderness guide and author of *Soulcraft*) believes that improvements will only flow once we progress from egocentric, competitive consumer societies to ecocentric, soul-based ones that are sustainable, cooperative and compassionate. He offers a practical integration of personal and spiritual understandings (from nature and the journey of the human soul) that will allow us to transform our culture.
ISBN 978 1876451 936

Spiritual Compass
The three qualities of life
Satish Kumar

Satish Kumar contends that spirituality must be part of our everyday existence - and so be present in business, relationships and daily life. Drawing on the Indian Ayurvedic tradition, he shows us how to recover the art of living with calmness, clarity and simplicity - and so have a peaceful and contented existence.
ISBN 978 1876451 943

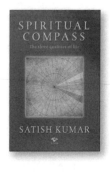

My People's Dreaming
An Aboriginal elder speaks on life, land, spirit and forgiveness
Max Dulumunmun Harrison

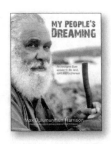

'Uncle' Max, as he is widely known, has been sharing his cultural knowledge for over 30 years. *My People's Dreaming* is drawn from extensive interviews with Uncle Max, who takes the reader through a description of the Creation story in Yuin culture. Through photos and words he reveals the significance of the giant stone beings on top of Gulaga, the sacred mountain that has now been returned to the custodianship of his people.
ISBN: 9781876451967

Mindfully Green
A personal and spiritual guide to whole-earth thinking
Stephanie Kaza

In this wise and compassionate book (full of 'all the impossibly gnarly problems that face us on this planet'), Stephanie Kaza helps awaken in the reader a state of 'green practice'. Her wise insights help us discover new ways to think more deeply about our impact on the natural world, engage in environmental change, and make green living a personal practice based in compassion and true conviction.
ISBN: 9781921462092

Stories of Belonging
Finding where your true self lives
Edited by Kali Wendorf

In *Stories of Belonging*, fifteen writers reveal their moments of finding where they truly belonged – be that in nature, to a community, a home, to their roots of family or people, or a culture they had to flee from or unexpectedly adapt to.
ISBN: 9781921462085